YOUR KNOWLEDGE HAS VALUE

Bibliographic information published by the German National Library:

The German National Library lists this publication in the National Bibliography; detailed bibliographic data are available on the Internet at http://dnb.dnb.de .

Imprint:

Copyright © 2018 GRIN Verlag
Print and binding: Books on Demand GmbH, Norderstedt Germany
ISBN: 9783668771130

This book at GRIN:

https://www.grin.com/document/435037

Palaniappan Sellappan

Learn Python. The Easy Way

Through Examples

GRIN Verlag

GRIN - Your knowledge has value

Since its foundation in 1998, GRIN has specialized in publishing academic texts by students, college teachers and other academics as e-book and printed book. The website www.grin.com is an ideal platform for presenting term papers, final papers, scientific essays, dissertations and specialist books.

Visit us on the internet:

http://www.grin.com/

http://www.facebook.com/grincom

http://www.twitter.com/grin_com

LEARN PYTHON
THE EASY WAY - THROUGH EXAMPLES

PROF. DR. P. SELLAPPAN

MALAYSIA UNIVERSITY
of Science and Technology

Preface

Python, developed by Guido van Rossum of Netherlands in the late 80s, and named after the BBC TV show Monty Python's Flying Circus, is one of the most user-friendly and powerful general-purpose computer programming languages available today.

Its English-like syntax makes it a great language for teaching and learning computer programming. Python's powerful data structures/types such as lists, tuples, dictionaries, sets, and arrays make coding simple. It also comes with an extensive collection of built-in/library functions that allows users to develop software applications with relative ease. Besides, users can freely import external modules to help them develop all sorts of applications.

Python's interactive and interpreted mode makes coding and testing software easy. Python also doubles us as a powerful and sophisticated calculator.

You can use Python to develop all sorts of applications ranging from simple Mathematical and Text processing to Database, Web, Graphical User Interface, Network, Games, Data Mining, Artificial Intelligence, Machine Learning and Deep Learning.

This book is intended for beginners who have little or no knowledge of programming. It is also suitable for intermediate programmers who already have some knowledge of programming.

This text is suitable for secondary school, college and university students irrespective of their field of study – be it Arts, Business, Science, Engineering, Life Sciences or Medicine. It starts with the basics, but progresses rapidly to the advanced topics such as lists, tuples, dictionaries, arrays, functions, classes, files and databases. So whether you are a beginner or an intermediate programmer, this book will help you master the essentials of Python programming very quickly.

The book is written in a simple, easy-to-read style and contains numerous examples to illustrate the programming concepts presented. It also contains exercises to test the reader's grasp of the material presented in each chapter.

Acknowledgements

I would like to gratefully acknowledge the contributions of several people who have in one or another assisted me in the preparation of this book. I would like to thank all my IT students and colleagues for their valuable input and feedback in the preparation of this manuscript.

My grateful thanks also go to Professor Dr. Premkumar Rajagopal, President of the Malaysia University of Science and Technology for giving me the opportunity, freedom, encouragement and support that I needed in the preparation of this manuscript. I would like to especially thank him for creating and nurturing an environment that actively promotes learning, research, teamwork and personal development. His dynamic leadership is greatly appreciated.

Last but first I would like to thank God for giving me the desire, motivation, interest, passion, strength and guidance to successfully complete this manuscript.

Dr. P. Sellappan
Professor of Information Technology
Dean of School of Science and Engineering
Provost of Malaysia University of Science and Technology

About the Author

Dr. P. Sellappan is currently Professor of Information Technology, Dean of School of Science and Engineering, and Provost of the Malaysia University of Science and Technology. Prior to joining Malaysia University of Science and Technology, he held a similar academic position in the Faculty of Computer Science and Information Technology, University of Malaya, Malaysia.

He holds a Bachelor in Economics degree with a Statistics major from the University of Malaya, a Master in Computer Science from the University of London (UK), and a PhD in Interdisciplinary Information Science from the University of Pittsburgh (USA).

Working in the academia for more than 30 years, he has taught a wide range of courses both at undergraduate and postgraduate levels: Principles of Programming, Advanced Programming, Programming Languages, Data Structures and Algorithms, System Analysis and Design, Software Engineering, Human Computer Interaction, Database Systems, Data Mining, Health Informatics, Web Applications, E-Commerce, Operating Systems, Management Information Systems, Research Methods, Mathematics and Statistics.

Professor Sellappan is an active researcher. He has received several national research grants from the Ministry of Science and Technology and Innovation under E-Science and FRGS to undertake IT-related research projects. Arising from these projects, he has published numerous research papers in reputable international journals and conference proceedings. Besides, he has also authored over a dozen college- and university-level IT text books.

As a thesis supervisor, he has supervised more than 70 Master and PhD theses. He also serves in editorial/review boards of several international journals and conferences. He is also chief editor of the Journal of Advanced Applied Sciences and the Plain Truth magazine. He is a certified trainer, external examiner, moderator and program assessor for IT programs for several local and international universities.

Together with other international experts, he has also served as an IT Consultant for several local and international agencies such as the Asian Development Bank, the United Nations Development Program, the World Bank, and the Government of Malaysia. His professional affiliation includes membership in the Chartered Engineering Council (UK), the British Computer Society (UK), the Institute of Statisticians (UK), and the Malaysian National Computer Confederation (MNCC).

Contents

Chapter 1

About Python

Learning Outcomes:

After completing this chapter, the student will be able to

- *Describe the main features of Python.*
- *Explain the Python environment.*
- *Run Python in calculator, interpreted, and script mode.*
- *Describe the different parts of a Python program.*

1.1 Python Features

Python was developed by Guido van Rossum of Netherlands in the late 80s. It was named after the BBC TV show <u>Monty Python's Flying Circus</u>.

Python is one of the popular general-purpose programming languages available today. Its English-like syntax makes it easier to learn. It is a great language for learning and teaching computer programming.

With Python you can develop all kinds of applications ranging from simple Business, Mathematical and Text processing to Database, Web, GUI (Graphical User Interface), Network, Games, Data Mining and Machine Learning applications.

Python has rich features which includes the following:

- Python can be used as a powerful and sophisticated calculator.

- Python is interactive – you can type your code at the Command prompt and view the results immediately.

- Python has an interpreter that lets you execute code as you type. You don't have to compile the whole program to run it. This is very useful for testing and debugging code.

- Python is object-oriented – you can define classes by bundling data attributes (variables) and functionality (methods) and create objects and work with them.

1) It has extensive libraries with built-in functions/methods that greatly simplify programming.

2) It is portable – you can run Python code on several hardware and software platforms (Linux and Windows).

3) It provides interfaces to major database software like MS Access, SQL Server, SQL Lite, MySQL and Oracle.

4) It supports Graphical User Interface (GUI).

5) It provides advanced data structures/types like lists, tuples, dictionaries and sets that make programming easy.

6) It supports automatic garbage collection to reclaim and reuse unused memory previously allocated to objects that no longer exist.

7) It can be used as a scripting language – you can write programs and store them in files for later use or embedding them in other programs.

1.2 Python Environment

You can run Python on several platforms like Windows and Linux. You can also incorporate Python code in programming languages like C, C++, Java and R.

You can execute Python code in three modes:

- **Calculator mode** – execute one statement or line of code at a time. It will automatically remember the previous results stored in the memory (provided they are not overwritten).

- **Interpreted mode** - you can execute statements and view the results immediately. You don't have to have the full program to execute it. This feature is very useful for testing and debugging code.

- **Script mode** – after you have debugged a program, you can store it in a file and later execute it as a script. This will improve performance, especially if it is a large or computationally-intensive program.

Thus Python provides a user-friendly environment for both novice, intermediate, and expert programmers.

1.3 Installing Python on Windows

This text is based on Python 3.6.x. for Windows. You can download and install Python as follows:

- Open a Web browser and go tohttps://www.anaconda.com/download/.

- Click on Download Python 3.6.x. for Windows.

- Run the downloaded file by accepting all the default settings.

- Run Python and you will see the Command window like the one shown below.

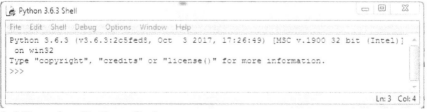

1.4 Running Python Code

You can run Python in three modes as follows:

- **Interactive Interpreter**

Enter `python` at the command line as follows:

```
C:> python
```

You can include options at the Command prompt such as

```
-d      provides debug output
file    runs script from file
```

- **Script at Command-line**

You can execute a Python script at the Command line as follows:

```
C:> python script.py
```

- **Integrated Development Environment**

You can also run Python in the Integrated Development Environment (IDE) that looks like the one shown below:

The IDE provides several windows to help you code, see output/results and consult related documentation if you need them. It also provides several menus and menu icons (Save, Run, Debug, Stop Debugging, etc.) at the top to help you write, test and debug code.

1.5 Sample Runs

Let's now run some simple code in the different modes.

Calculator Mode

At the >>> prompt, type the code below and press Enter.

```
>>> print ('Hello world!')
```

You will get the following output:

```
Hello world!
```

Here are more examples with their output.

```
>>> print ('John ' + 'Mark')  # join the two names
John Mark

>>> 5 + 7 * 7
54

>>> 15/3 + 5 * 3 - 12
8.0

>>> math.sqrt(25)  # take the square root of 25
5.0

>>> math.sqrt(25+24)
7.0

>>> print (5 + math.sqrt(49))
12.0

>>> v = ['Wong', 'Sally', 'Ali', 'Sam'] # a list of names
>>> print (v)
['Wong', 'Sally', 'Ali', 'Sam']

>>> t = ('red', 'yellow', 'green')       # a tuple of colors
>>> print (t)
('red', 'yellow', 'green')

>>> d = {'Sam': 111, 'Sally': 222} # a dictionary of paired items
>>> print (d)
{'Sam': 111, 'Sally': 222}
```

Interpreted Mode

Type the following code and run by clicking the arrow button on the menu bar (▶).

```
import math
name = 'Sally'
age = 25
print ('\nYour name is {} and you are {} years old.'.format(name, age))
```

```
x = 5
y = 44
print ('\nSquare root of x+y = ', math.sqrt(x+y))
```

You will get the following output:

```
Your name is Sally and you are 25 years old.

Square root of x+y =   7.0
```

Script Mode

Write a Python script (like the above) and store it in the default directory as `test.py`. (Python files have extension `.py`).

You can now run the stored script by typing

```
$ python test.py
```

The script will produce the same output as above.

1.6 Parts of a Python Program

A Python program has many parts/sections (see the below sample program): comments, expressions, statements, input, output, functions, import, etc. We will explain the different parts of a Python program using a simple sample program given below.

Note: The line numberings on the left, generated by the system, is for reference purpose only – they are not part of the code. Also, for easy reading, Python uses different colors for different parts of a program: green for comments, blue for keywords, pink for functions, etc.

Comments

Inserting comments in a program makes the code more readable. You can insert comments on a single line, on several lines, or inline after a statement.

A single line comment starts with a sharp character (#) as in lines 7, 10.... in the sample code. Everything on that after # is treated as a comment. You can create a *multiline* comment by starting *each* line with a #.

An *inline* comment starts with a # *after* a statement as in lines 12, 17.... in the sample code.

You can also insert a multiline comment by starting and ending the comment with triple apostrophes (' ' '). Such a comment can span several lines as in lines 2 to 6.

Line spacing

Inserting blank lines to separate code blocks makes a program more readable as in lines 9, 14....

Indentation

Code blocks in Python are *indented* by a fixed number of spaces (typically 4 spaces) as in lines 12 and 13. All statements in the code block must follow the *same* indentation.

5

Sample Python code

```
 1 # -*- coding: utf-8 -*-
 2 """
 3 Created on Sat Jan 13 16:13:08 2018
 4
 5 @author: sel1780
 6 """
 7 # import math functions from system library
 8 import math
 9
10 # define function to calculate area of a circle given its radius
11 def cir_area(radius):
12     area = math.pi * radius * radius  # pi is from math library
13     return area
14
15 # input radius from keyboard, then convert the value to float
16 r = float(input('Enter radius: '))
17 a = cir_area(r)  # call cir_area function with radius r
18 # print/display output
19 print ('\nArea of circle with radius {:.2f} = {:.2f}'.format(r, a))
20
21 # calculate area of triangle given its base and height
22 base = 5.8
23 height = 7.2
24 tri_area = 0.5 * base * height
25 print ('\nArea of triangle with base {:.2f} and height {:.2f} = {:.2f}'.\
26         format(base, height, tri_area))
27
28 name = ['Joe', 'May', 'Wong']
29 print ('\nName list:', name)
30
31 color = ('red', 'yellow', 'green')
32 print ('\nTraffic light colors: ', color)
33
34 tel = {'Joe': 1234567, 'May': 2345678, 'Wong': 3456789}
35 print ('\nTel. list: ', tel)
36
```

Sample output

```
Enter radius: 5.85

Area of circle with radius 5.85 = 107.51

Area of triangle with base 5.80 and height 7.20 = 20.88

Name list: ['Joe', 'May', 'Wong']

Traffic light colors:  ('red', 'yellow', 'green')

Tel. list:  {'Joe': 1234567, 'May': 2345678, 'Wong': 3456789}
```

Keywords

Keywords (also called reserved words) have special meaning in Python. You cannot use these keywords for any other purpose such as for naming identifiers (variables, functions or classes). For example, `import` (line 8), `define` (line 11) and `return` (line 13) in the code are keywords.

Case sensitivity

Python identifiers for naming variables, functions and classes are *case-sensitive*. It treats uppercase and lowercase letters as *different* characters. That means, `name`, `Name` and `NAME` are all different identifiers.

Parameters

Parameters (arguments) in functions (methods) are enclosed between a pair of curved brackets `()`. The brackets are still needed even if a function has no parameters.

Input statement

The `input` statement (function) is used for reading data from the Keyboard (or Console). It takes the form

```
variable = input ('prompt')
```

where `variable` stores the data entered, and `prompt` prompts the user to enter the data.

Output statement

The `print` function is used for sending output (results) to the monitor (Console). It takes the form

```
print (output list)
```

where `output list` is a list of variables or expressions that you want to print or display.

Assignment statement

An assignment statement takes the form

```
variable = expression
```

where `variable` stores the result of the `expression`, and `=` is an assignment operator (not an equality operator). In an assignment statement, the expression on the right-hand side of `=` is first evaluated and the result is assigned to the `variable` on the left-hand side of `=`. The `expression` can be a number, a constant, a literal, a variable, an algebraic expression, or a function or method call.

Import statement

The `import` statement is used to import modules (classes) stored in external files. It begins with the keyword `import` followed by the name of the module (e.g. `math`) as in line 8.

Lists, tuples and dictionaries

Python variables include *grouped data*: lists, tuples and dictionaries. Lists are enclosed between square brackets `[]` as in line 28; tuples are enclosed between curved brackets `()` as in line 31; and dictionaries (containing paired items) are enclosed between braces or curly brackets `{}` as in line 34.

Note: We will discuss all these and topics in greater detail in the rest of the chapters. So don't worry if you haven't fully grasped the material presented in this chapter. The sample code is meant to give you a flavor of how a Python program looks like. As you progress through the chapters, you will learn how to write Python programs.

Exercise

1. Run Python in calculator mode to evaluate the following:

   a) $23 - (4 * 15) / 3 + 73$
   b) Concatenate (join) the strings "Good" and "day"
   c) Concatenate the strings "time", "and", "chance"

2. Run Python in calculator mode to evaluate the following:

   a) Square of 547.25
   b) Square root of 973.16
   c) Square root of (973.75 + square of (45))

3. Run Python in interpreted mode to execute the following code:

```
x = (55 + 25) * 2
y = 546.95 + sqrt(25)
z = x + y
print ('Sum of x and y = ', z)
```

4. Execute the code in question (3) in script mode.

5. Run Python in interpreted mode to execute the following code:

```
hours = 98
rate = 35.70
gross_pay = hours * rate
deduction = 10 * pay
net_pay = pay - deduction
print ('Take home pay = $', netpay)
```

6. Execute the code in question (5) in script mode.

Chapter 2

Python Basics

Learning Outcomes:

After completing this chapter, the student will be able to

- *Form identifiers and variables.*
- *Use arithmetic, logical and relational operators.*
- *Form expressions.*
- *Write assignment statements.*
- *Identify different data types.*
- *Perform input/output.*
- *Write simple Python code.*

2.1 Identifiers

Identifiers are used to name variables, functions, classes, objects and modules. They are simply references (pointers) to memory locations for storing objects such as numbers, strings, dates or Boolean values.

An identifier consists of one or more lower and upper letters (a-z, A-Z), digits (0-9) and the underscore (_). Identifiers must start with an underscore or a letter followed by zero or more letters, digits or underscores. Special characters such as #, &, @, $ and % are not allowed in an identifier. The blank or space character is also not allowed in an identifier.

Python identifiers are *case-sensitive*, meaning it treats uppercase and lowercase letters as different characters. That means, NAME, Name and name are all different identifiers.

The following naming convention is used for identifiers:

- All class names start with uppercase letters.
- All other identifiers start with lowercase letters.
- An identifier with a single leading underscore indicates that it is private.
- An identifier with two leading underscores indicates that it is strongly private.
- An identifier that ends with two trailing underscores indicates that it is a special language-defined name.

The following are examples of valid identifiers.

```
k                 rate_of_return      Employee        x
count             total_salary        suffix_         match
name              __init__            Account         found
_prefix           sum_of_x2           tax_rate_1      email
age               interest_rate       city            myList
```

The following are examples of invalid identifiers.

Invalid identifier	Reason
rate 5.5	Contains embedded blank and period (.)
tel.list	Contains embedded period.
123	Doesn't start with letter or underscore (_)
#employees	Contains invalid character (#).
@email	Contain invalid character (@).
gross_salary_$	Contains invalid character ($).
x@gmail.com	Contains invalid characters (@ and .).
x.y.z	Contains invalid character (.).
a, b, c	Contains invalid characters (blank and ,).
my name	Contains embedded blank.
x-y-z	Contains invalid character (−).
1account	Starts with a digit (1).
*prefix	Contains invalid character (*).
my account	Contains embedded blank.
###varx	Contains invalid character (#).
5lists	Starts with a digit (1).
$deposit	Contains invalid character ($).
!#Python	Contains invalid characters (! and #).
percent%	Contains invalid character (%).

2.2 Keywords

Keywords, also called reserved words, have special meaning in Python. You cannot use them for any other purpose, e.g. for naming identifiers, variables, functions, classes, objects or modules. All keywords use only *lowercase* letters.

Below is a list of Python keywords.

```
and         as          assert      break       class
continue    def         del         elif        else
except      exec        finally     for         from
global      if          import      in          is
lambda      not         or          pass        print
raise       return      try         while       with
yield
```

2.3 Variables

Unlike in some other programming languages (like C# and Java), Python variables don't need explicit declaration. Python automatically allocates memory to variables when you assign them values. The amount of memory Python allocates to variables will depend on their data type. Some data types (e.g. float) will require more bytes than others (e.g. integer).

Variables are pointers (references) to data objects such as integers, float, strings, Boolean, list, tuple and dictionary.

For example:

n = 12 would be represented internally as follows:

n  12

10

Similarly,

`price = 29.90` would be represented internally as follows (float type requires more bytes):

price  | 29.90 |

`sentence = 'It is gorgeous day!'`

would be represented internally as follows (the number of bytes needed will depend on the length of the string):

sentence ─────────────────────→ | It is gorgeous day! |

2.4 Comments

Comments are inserted into a program to make it readable. The Python interpreter does not process comments – it just ignores them.

Comments start with a sharp sign (#). Characters following # are part of a comment. You can create a multiline comment by starting each line with #. You can also insert a comment *after* a statement on the *same* line. This is called an *inline* comment.

Here are some examples of valid comments.

```
#!/usr/bin/python
# -*- coding: utf-8 -*-
# this is line1
# this is line2
# all the above form a multiline comment

print ('Hello, Python!')  # this is an inline comment
```

2.5 Quotes

Quotes are used to indicate literal strings. You can use a single ('), double (") or triple (' ' ') quote to indicate a string literal as long as it begins and ends with the *same* quote type. The triple quote is used to span a long quote (a sentence or a paragraph) across multiple lines.

The following are examples of valid quotes.

```
'word'

"This is a sentence."

""" This is a valid quote """

"She said, 'I am not confused.'"
"""
Spyder Editor

This is a temporary script file.
"""

"""
```

11

```
    This is a paragraph. It is made up of
    multiple lines and sentences. This is line 2
    and this is line 3.
"""
```

The following are examples of invalid quotes.

```
'I am really confused."                      # different quote types

"She said, 'I am confused too."'             # quote type not matching

"""Why everyone says, 'I am confused!"'      # quote type not matching
```

2.6 Blank Lines & Indentation

A blank line is one that contains only whitespaces. Python ignores blank lines. Blank lines are inserted to separate code blocks and thus make the code readable.

Unlike in some other programming languages such as C# and Java, Python doesn't use braces or curly brackets ({}) to separate code blocks. Instead, it uses line indentation. The number of spaces in a line indentation can vary, but all statements within a code block must have the *same* indentation (typically four spaces).

The following line indentation is valid as all statements in the code blocks follow the same number of spaces.

```
if True:
    print ("True")  # this statement is indented by 4 spaces
else:
    print ("False") # this is also indented by 4 spaces
```

The following indentation is invalid as the statements in the code blocks do not follow the indentation rule.

```
if True:
    print ("Answer")    # indented by 4 spaces
    print ("True")
else:
      print ("Answer")  # wrong - not indented by 4 spaces
      print ("False")
```

All continuous lines indented with the *same* number of spaces constitute a code block.

2.7 Multi-Line Statements

Typically, each statement ends with a new line. However, if a statement is long, you can use the continuation character (\) to indicate that the statement continues on the next line. For example:

```
total = item_one + \ # this statement continues on the next line
        item_two + \ # this also continues on the next line
        item_three
```

No line continuation character is needed for items that appear in square brackets [], curved brackets (), or curly brackets {} as in the following code:

```
# the following doesn't require the line continuation character '\'

days = ['Monday', 'Tuesday', 'Wednesday',
```

```
                'Thursday', 'Friday']

dict = {key1: value1, key2: value2, key3: value3,
        key4, value4, key5:value5}

colors = ('violet', 'indigo', 'blue', 'green',
          'yellow', 'red', 'orange')
```

2.8 Operators

Python supports the following operators.

- Arithmetic operators
- Comparison/Relational operators
- Assignment operators
- Logical operators
- Bitwise operators
- Membership operators
- Identity operators

Arithmetic Operators

Arithmetic operators are similar to those used in algebra except for *, **, % and //.

The table below gives the list of arithmetic operators. The last column gives examples for the operands: x = 10 and y = 20.

Operator	Meaning	Description	Example
+	Addition	Adds values on either side of the operator.	x + y = 30
−	Subtraction	Subtracts right hand operand from left hand.	x − y = −10
*	Multiplication	Multiplies values on either side of the operator.	x * y = 200
/	Division	Divides left hand operand by right hand operand.	y / x = 2
%	Modulus	Divides left hand operand by right hand operand and returns remainder.	y % a = 0
**	Exponentiation	Performs exponential calculation on operators.	x**y =10²⁰
//	Floor division	Divides the operands and gets the quotient. But if one of the operands is negative, the result is floored, i.e., rounded away from zero (towards negative infinity).	9//2 = 4 9.0//2.0 = 4.0 −11//3 = −4 11.0//3 = −4.0

Logical Operators

Logical operators are and (&), or (|) and not.

The table below gives the list of logical operators. The last column gives examples for the operands: x = True and y = False.

Operator	Meaning	Description	Example
& (and)	AND	Adds values on either side of the operator.	x and y = False x & y = False
| (or)	OR	Subtracts right hand operand from left hand.	x or y = True x | y = True
not	NOT	Multiplies values on either side of the operator.	not x = False not y = True

Comparison Operators

The comparison or relational operators compare the values of the two operands and yields the result of the comparison which is True or False.

The table below gives the list of comparison operators. The last column gives examples for the operands: x = 10 and y = 20.

Operator	Meaning	Description	Example
==	Equal	If the values of two operands are equal, then the condition becomes true.	x == y yields False
!=	Not equal	If values of two operands are not equal, then condition becomes true.	x != y yields True
<>	Not equal	If values of two operands are not equal, then condition becomes true.	x <> y yields True
>	Greater than	If the value of left operand is greater than the value of right operand, then condition becomes true.	x > y yields False
<	Less than	If the value of left operand is less than the value of right operand, then condition becomes true.	x < y yields True
>=	Greater than or equal to	If the value of left operand is greater than or equal to the value of right operand, then condition becomes true.	x >= y yields False
<=	Less than or equal to	If the value of left operand is less than or equal to the value of right operand, then condition becomes true.	x <= y yields True

Assignment Operators

Assignment operators evaluate the expression on the right-hand side of = and assign the result to the variable on the left-hand side. Some assignment operators are short-hand operators that use the left-hand operand as part of the expression.

The table below gives the list of assignment operators. The last column gives examples for the operands: x = 10 and y = 20.

Operator	Meaning	Description	Example
=	Assign	Assigns values from right side operands to left side operand	x = y Assigns 20 to x
+=	Add and assign	It adds right operand to the left operand and assign the result to left operand	x += y (same as x = x + y) Assigns 30 to x
-=	Subtract and assign	It subtracts right operand from the left operand and assign the result to left operand	x -= y (same as x = x - y) Assigns -10 to x

	Multiply and assign	It multiplies right operand with the left operand and assign the result to left operand	`x *= y (same as x = x * y )` `Assigns 200 to x`
`*=`			
`/=`	Divide and assign	It divides left operand with the right operand and assign the result to left operand	`x /= y(same as x = x / y)` `Assigns 0.5 to x`
`%=`	Modulus and assign	It takes modulus using two operands and assign the result to left operand	`x % y (same as x = x / y)` `Assigns 10 to x`
`**=`	Exponent and assign	Performs exponential (power) calculation on operators and assign value to the left operand	`x **= y (same as x = x ** y)` `Assigns 10`^{20}` to x`
`//=`	Floor and assign	It performs floor division on operators and assign value to the left operand	`x //= y (same as x = x / y)` `Assigns 0 to x`

Bitwise Operators

Bitwise operators perform bit-by-bit operation.

The table below gives the list of bitwise operators. The last column gives examples for the operands: x = 15 and y = 23. The binary equivalent of x and y are as follows:

```
x = 0b1111
y = 0b1100001
```

Operator	Meaning	Description	Example
`&`	AND	Operator copies a bit to the result if it exists in both operands	`x & y` `= 0b1`
`|`	OR	It copies a bit if it exists in either operand.	`x	y` `= 0b1101111`
`^`	XOR	It copies the bit if it is set in one operand but not both.	`x ^ y` `= 0b1101110`
`~`	Ones Complement	It is unary and has the effect of 'flipping' bits.	`~x` `= -0b10000`
`<<`	Left shift	The left operands value is moved left by the number of bits specified by the right operand.	`x << 2` `= 0b111100`
`>>`	Right shift	The left operands value is moved right by the number of bits specified by the right operand.	`x >> 2` `= 0b11`

Membership Operators

Membership operators test if an item is a member of a sequence such as string, list or tuple.

There are two membership operators: in and not in as shown below. The last column gives examples for the operands: x, y and z:

```
x = 'jack and jill and sam'
y = ['jack', 'jill', 'sam']
z = ('red', 'blue', 'green')
v = [1, 2, 3, 4, 5]
```

Operator	Meaning	Description	Example

in	Is member?	Evaluates to true if it finds a variable in the specified sequence and false otherwise.	`'jill' in string x? True`
			`'jack' in list y? True`
			`'green' in z? True`
			`'yellow' in z? False`
			`5 in v? True`

not in	Is not member?	Evaluates to true if it does not finds a variable in the specified sequence and false otherwise.	`'sally' not in x? True`
			`'jack' not in y? False`
			`'blue' not in z? False`
			`2 not in v? False`

Identity Operators

Identity operators compare the memory locations of two objects.

There are two identity operators: is and is not as shown below. The last column gives examples for the operands:

```
x = 127
y = x
z = 256
```

Operator	Meaning	Description	Example

is	Is same memory?	Evaluates to True if operands point to the same object and False otherwise.	`id(x) == id(y)? True`
			`id(x) == id(z)? False`
			`x is y? True`
			`x is z? False`

is not	Is not same memory?	Evaluates to False if operands point to the same object and true otherwise.	`x is not y? False` `x is not z? True`

Operator Precedence

The table below lists the operator precedence from the highest to the lowest.

Operators	Description
`**`	Exponentiation (highest)
`~ + -`	Complement, unary plus and minus
`* / % //`	Multiply, divide, modulus and floor division
`+ -`	Addition and subtraction
`>> <<`	Right and left bitwise shift
`&`	Bitwise AND
`| ^`	Bitwise OR and exclusive OR
`<= < > >=`	Comparison operators
`<> == !=`	Equality operators
`= %= /= //= -= += *= **=`	Assignment operators
`is is not`	Identity operators
`in not in`	Membership operators
`and or not`	Logical operators (lowest)

16

2.9 Expressions

Expressions in Python are similar to algebraic expressions in math except for certain operators like *, **, %, and //.

Here are some examples of valid expressions.

```
5
2 + 10/5 - 20
7 + (2 * 6) - (45/9)
3 ** 2 + (17 % 12) - (12 // 4)
(98 - (45 + 7) - (12 * 3) + (66 / 3))
True
'color'
''brilliant piece''
```

2.10 Assignment Statements

The assignment operator (=) is used to assign values to variables. It takes the form

```
variable = expression
```

The `variable` on the left hand side of the assignment operator stores the value of the `expression` on the right hand side.

Here are some examples (code snippets) of assignment statements.

```
product = 'iPhone10'    # assign a string
price = 1200.55         # assign a number with a decimal point
quantity = 5            # assign an integer
order_status = True     # assign a Boolean value
print ('Product: ', product )
print ('Price: $', price)
print ('Quantity: ', quantity)
print ('Order status: ', order_status)
```

The above code will produce the following output:

```
Product:  iPhone10
Price: $ 1200.55
Quantity:  5
Order status:  True
```

2.11 Multiple Assignments in a Single Statement

Python allows you to make multiple assignments in a single statement. For example, the code below assigns the value 1 to the variables a, b and c simultaneously.

```
a = b = c = 1
```

The statement creates an integer object with value 1, and all the variables point to the *same* object. There is only one copy of 1.

Python also allows you to assign multiple values to multiple variables in a single statement as in the code below.

17

```
product, price, quantity = 'iPad', 1200.50, 5
```

Here, iPad is assigned to product; 1200.50 is assigned to price; and 5 is assigned to quantity. The values on the right hand side are assigned to the variables on the left hand side in the *same* order.

2.12 Multiple Statements in a Single Line

Python allows multiple statements on a single line (this saves space), separated by a semicolon (;) provided no statement starts a new code block. Here is an example.

```
x = 5; y = 7; z = x + y; print ('z = ', z)
```

The above code has four statements – all packed compactly in one line.

2.13 Code Blocks

A code block is a collection of one or more statements all following the same line indentation. Compound statements like if, while, def or class have headers. A header begins the statement with a keyword and terminates with a colon (:). The colon marks the beginning of a new code block as shown in the code below.

```
if expression:
    code block     # indented
elif expression:
    code block     # must follow the above indentation
else:
    code block     # must also follow the same indentation
```

2.14 Data Types

Python has several data types: number, string, Boolean, list, tuple, dictionary and set.

The number data type stores numerical values such as integer and floating point numbers. String data type stores a sequence of characters. Boolean data type stores the value True or False. List data type stores a list of (mutable) items enclosed between []. Tuple data type stores a list of (immutable) items enclosed between (). Dictionary data type stores a list of (mutable) paired items in the form of key:value enclosed between {}. A set data has a collection of items which can be any data type.

Mutable items can be changed or updated; *immutable* items cannot be changed or updated. All single-item variables are mutable. Some group-item variables like lists and dictionaries are mutable. Tuples, however, are immutable.

Here are some examples of data types and their internal representation.

```
item = 'iPad'  # creates string object iPad; then item points to iPad
itemcopy = item

price = 1200.50
quantity = 5

names = ['Joe', 'Sam', 'May']
```

```
colors= ('G', 'Y', 'R')

tel = {'Joe': 111, 'Sam': 222, 'May':333}
mytel = tel
```

When objects of these data types are created and assigned to variables, the variables point to these objects. Internally, the above assignments look something like this:

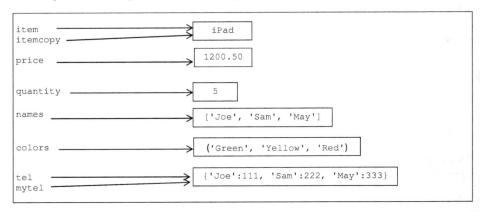

You can delete references to objects using the del statement as in the code below.

```
del itemcopy, mytel
```

Numbers

Python supports four number types:

- int (signed integers)
- long (long integers, which can also be represented in octal and hexadecimal)
- float (floating point real values)
- complex (complex numbers)

Here are some examples of number types.

int	long	float	complex
523	28974L	3.1412	2.172j
−987	567L	999.99	0.765j
0x45	−123L	−789.8	9.453J
−123	1234567L	2.45E5	−52345j
5000	0xABC1	−15.5e12	5+45j

- Python allows you to use a lowercase l with long, but it is strongly recommended that you use only an uppercase L to avoid confusion with the number 1. It displays long integers with an uppercase L.

- A complex number consists of an ordered pair of real floating-point numbers denoted by x + yj, where x and y are the real numbers and j is the imaginary unit.

19

Strings

A string is a sequence of characters enclosed between a pair of quotation marks of the *same* type. Python allows you to use a single (') or double (' ') quote. You cannot mix the quote for the same string.

You can get subsets of strings from a string by using the slice operator ([ ] or [:]) with indexes. Index always starts with a 0 at the beginning of a string. Index can also start with −1 at the end of the string.

The plus sign (+) in the string acts as a concatenation (join) operator and the asterisk (∗) acts as a repetition operator.

Here are some examples.

```
str = 'Hello World!'
print str                  # prints the whole string
print str[0]               # prints first character of the string
print str[2:5]             # prints characters starting from 3rd to 5th
print str[2:]              # prints characters starting from 3rd character
print str * 2              # prints the string two times
print str + ' Test'        # prints concatenated string
```

The above code produces the following output:

```
Hello World!
H
llo
llo World!
Hello World!Hello World!
Hello World! Test
```

Lists

A list contains (mutable) items separated by commas and enclosed within square brackets ([ ]). They are similar to arrays, but list items need not be of the same data type.

Like strings, you can access list items using the slice operator ([ ] and [:]).

Here are some examples.

```
list = ['iPhone 10', 500.00, 'black']
list2 = ['john', 'sally']
print (list)               # prints complete list
print (list[0])            # prints first element of the list
print (list[1:3])          # prints elements starting from 2nd till 3rd
print (list[2:])           # prints elements starting from 3rd element
print (list2 * 2)          # prints list two times
print (list + list2)       # prints concatenated lists
```

The above code produces the following output:

```
['iPhone 10', 500.0, 'black']
iPhone 10
[500.0, 'black']
['black']
['john', 'sally', 'john', 'sally']
['iPhone 10', 500.0, 'black', 'john', 'sally']
```

You can add, delete or change items in a list.

Tuples

Tuples items are immutable – they cannot be changed. Tuple items are separated by commas and enclosed within curved brackets (( )).

The main difference between a list and tuple is that list items can be updated whereas tuple items cannot be updated. Tuples can be thought of as *read-only* lists.

Like lists, you can access tuple items using the slice operator ([ ] and [:]).

Here are some examples.

```
colors = ('violet', 'indigo', 'blue', 'green', 'yellow', 'red', 'orange')
print (colors)          # prints complete list
print (colors [0])      # prints first element of the list
print (colors [1:3])    # prints elements starting from 2nd till 3rd
print (colors [2:])     # prints elements starting from 3rd element
print (colors * 2)      # prints list two times
```

The above code produces the following output:

```
('violet', 'indigo', 'blue', 'green', 'yellow', 'red', 'orange')
violet
('indigo', 'blue')
('blue', 'green', 'yellow', 'red', 'orange')
('violet', 'indigo', 'blue', 'green', 'yellow', 'red', 'orange', 'violet',
'indigo', 'blue', 'green', 'yellow', 'red', 'orange')
```

You *cannot* add, delete or change tuple items. The following code, for example, is invalid.

```
colors [2] = 'magenta'    # invalid as tuple is immutable
colors [] = ' '
del colors [4]
```

Dictionaries

A dictionary contains a collection of *paired* items in the form of key: value and enclosed within braces or curly brackets ({ }). The items in a dictionary can be strings or numbers.

Dictionary items are accessed by their key values or by using functions like keys() and values() as shown in the code below.

```
d = {'my': 'malaysia', 'fr': 'france', 'sg': 'singapore', 'vn': 'vietnam'}
print (d['vn'])
print (d.keys())        # print the keys
print (d.values())      # print the values
print (d.keys(), d.values())  # print keys and values

del d['vn']             # delete {'vn': 'vietnam'} from list
print (d)
d['ng'] = 'nigeria'     # append {'ng': 'nigeria'} to list
print (d)
d.clear()               # clear all items
print (d)
```

21

The above code produces the following output:

```
dict_keys(['my', 'fr', 'sg', 'vn'])
dict_values(['malaysia', 'france', 'singapore', 'vietnam'])
dict_keys(['my', 'fr', 'sg', 'vn']) dict_values(['malaysia', 'france',
'singapore', 'vietnam'])
{'my': 'malaysia', 'fr': 'france', 'sg': 'singapore'}
{'my': 'malaysia', 'fr': 'france', 'sg': 'singapore', 'ng': 'nigeria'}
{}
```

Note that dictionary items are *unordered*, so the concept of order doesn't arise.

2.15 Input/Output Statements

The `input` statement (function) is used to read data from the Keyboard. It takes the form

```
variable = input ('prompt')
```

where `variable` stores the data entered, and `prompt` prompts the user to enter the data.

The statement terminates when the user presses the Enter key.

Here is an example.

```
x = input ('Enter a value: ')
```

`Enter a value` prompts the user to enter a value and x stores the value entered.

You can insert escape sequences inside an `input` function. For example, to display the prompt on a new line, you can use `'\n'` as in the following code:

```
y = input ('\nEnter a value: ')
```

The `print` function is used for displaying output (results) on the monitor. It takes the form

```
print (output-list)
```

where `output-list` is a list of variables or expressions that you want to print/display.

Here is an example.

```
x = 5
y = 7
print (x, y)
```

This will produce the flowing output.
```
5 7
```

You can also include labels and escape sequences within the `print` statement (function) as in the code below.

```
x = 5
y = 7
print ('x =', x, 'y =', y)
print ('x =', x, '\ty =', y)      # '\t' is the tab character
print ('\nx =', x, '\ny =', y)    # '\n' is the new line character
```
This will produce the following output.

```
x = 5 y = 7
x = 5    y = 7

x = 5
y = 7
```

2.16 Importing Modules

A typical Python program will include several standard library/built-in functions and methods to perform a variety of tasks such as getting the length of a string, converting data from one type to another, reading input form the keyboard, sending output to the monitor or file, etc.

However, Python doesn't provide all the functions that users will need. But there are many modules (also called classes) available on the Net that contain functions (also called methods) to perform all sorts of tasks – mathematical, statistical, random number generation, string processing, and plotting graphs. To use these functions, you need to import the modules (classes) that contain these functions.

The `import` statement takes the form

```
import module
```

For example, to import functions from math and random modules, you will use statements

```
import math
import random
```

To import a specific function, say randint from the random module, you will use the statement

```
from random import randint
```

where random is the module and randint is the function.

Exercise

1. List the Python data types.

2. Which of the following identifiers are invalid?

```
(a)   some-value
(b)   interest rate
(c)   roi%
(d)   $salary
(e)   cityName
(f)   net__pay
(g)   sum_of_x&y
(h)   123store
(i)   store123
(j)   #comment
(k)   _alias
(l)   __init__
```

3. Given $x = 10$, $y = 7$ and $z = 2$ which of the following expressions are False?

```
(a)  x > y + z
```

```
(b) z <= 7
(c) x == y
(d) x != z
(e) y + z <= x
(f) x - y > z
(g) x % y == 3
(h) z ** 2 > x
(i) -(-x - z) >= y
(j) x - y - x
```

4. Given integer variables x, y and z with values 10, 7, 2 respectively, write code to compute the value of each of the following arithmetic expressions:

```
(a) x + 2 * y - z
(b) x / z - (x * x + y)
(c) (x * y) % z
(d) 5 * (x + y + z) - x/z
(e) x * y - x * z
(f) y * (x + z) * (x - y)
```

5. Given integer variables a = 2, b = 5, c = 7 and floating-point variables x = 10.0, y = 10.5, z = 20.0, write code to obtain the correct result for each of the following expressions:

```
(a) y - a/b
(b) a - b * z / a)
(c) x - (b / a) * c
```

6. Using the values given in question 5, calculate the value of each of the following expressions:

```
(a) a++
(b) a < 2 && y > 5.0
(c) c >= a
(d) a < b || b > c
(e) z != 10.0
(f) a == 25
```

7. Given the following assignment statements:

```
i = 4, j = 21
x = 94.55
a = 'z', b = 't', c = ' '
p = q = r = 7
```

Determine the value of the variable on the left-hand side in the following statements:

```
(a) k = i * j
(b) y = x + i
(c) y = k = j
(d) a = b = c
(e) i += j
(f) j -= (k = 5)
(g) p + x - i
```

8. Which of the following comments are valid?

```
(a)   'majestic mountains'
(b)   "I can't believe that!'
(c)   'why don't you believe?"
(d)   """sure, things will be brighter next year" '
(e)   'that is not "what I really said"'
(f)   "it's OK, """is it really OK? """ "
```

9. Trace the output of the following code:

```
x = y = z = 57
a, b, c = 22, 33, 55
p, q = 22.35, 79.82
r1 = x + a
r2 = z + b
x = c + q
print (r1, r2, x)
```

10. Given x = 4, y = 21, z = 94.55, a = 'nice', b = 'meal', c = ' ', write to compute the following

```
z - 2 * (x + y)
a + c + b
a * 3
y % x + z
(a + c + b) * 3
((a + c + b + c + c)*3)
((a + c + b + c*2) * 3)
```

Chapter 3

Control Structures

Learning Outcomes:

After completing this chapter, the student will be able to

- *Explain control structures in programs.*
- *Use if, if...else, if...elif...else statements.*
- *Use for, for...else, while and while...else loops.*
- *Use range function.*
- *Use nested loop.s*
- *Use break, continue and pass statements.*

Control structure refers to the order of execution of instructions/statements in a computer program. Basically there are three types/structures of control flows: sequence, decision making and loop (also called repetition/ iteration). Besides these, there are also other control flows for exiting or continuing a loop before it ends normally.

3.1 Sequence

This is the simplest control flow structure. In this structure, statements are executed *sequentially* - one by one starting from the first to the last.

Here is an example.

```
# execute statements sequentially
x = 5
y = 7
z = x + y
print (z)
```

The above statements are executed in that order from x = 5 to print (z).

This control structure alone is insufficient to solve real-life problems. You need other control structures such as decision making and looping.

3.2 Decision Making

The decision control structure allows a program to branch off or jump to another section of the code based on a certain condition, for example, to display the grade Fail if a student's mark is less than 50 and the grade Pass if the mark is 50 or above.

This control flow comes in three forms:

```
1) if
2) if…else
3) if…elif…else
```

We will discuss each of these in the sequel.

- **if**

This type takes the form

```
if (expression):
    statement(s)   # code block
```

If the `expression` evaluates to `True`, the `statements` in the code block will be executed; otherwise, the `statements` will be skipped. Any `expression` that evaluates or takes a *non-zero* value is evaluated to `True`; otherwise, it is evaluated to `False`.

Here are some simple sample programs (code snippets).

Program (code snippet) 3.1 tests if x < y. Since it is `True`, it displays the message in the `print` statement. If the expression is y < x, nothing will be displayed because it will evaluate to `False`.

Program 3.1
```
# illustrates if statement
x = 5
y = 7
if (x < y):    # x < y evaluates to True
    print ('x is smaller than y')   # this will be executed
```

Output
```
x is smaller than y
```

Program 3.2 tests the expression x && y. Since it evaluate to `False`, there will be no output.

Program 3.2
```
x = True
y = False
if (x && y):    # x && y evaluates to False
    print ('both x and y are not True')   # this will not be executed
```

Output
[None]

Program 3.3 tests the compound expression x<y && p||q. Since it evaluates to `True`, it will output the message in the `print` statement.

Program 3.3
```
x, y = 5, 7 # multiple assignments: x = 5, y = 7
p = True
q = False
if (x < y && p || q):    # x < y and p || q both evaluate to True
    print ('The whole expression is true.')   # this will be executed
```

Output
```
The whole expression is true.
```

Program 3.4 tests if y evaluates to `True`. As y is not zero, it evaluates to `True`; so the code will display the message in the `print` statement.

Program 3.4
```
y = 5
if (y):    # y is not zero, so it evaluates to True
    print ('y evaluates to True')   # this will be executed
```

27

Output
```
y evaluates to True
```

Program 3.5 tests if x evaluates to True. As x is zero, it evaluates to False; so the code will not display the message in the first print statement. However, it will display the message in the second print statement because the string s evaluates to True.

Program 3.5
```
x = 0
if (x):  # x = 0 evaluates to False
    print ('False condition') # this will not execute
s = 'red'
if (s):  # s = 'red' evaluates to True
    print ('True condition')
```

Output
```
True condition
```

Program 3.6 will not display the message in the first print statement (as b is False) but will display the message in the second print statement (as speed > 110 is True).

Program 3.6
```
b = False
if (b):
    print ('This statement will not execute! ')
speed = 150
if (speed > 110):
    print ('You have committed a traffic offense! ')
```

Output
```
You have committed a traffic offense!
```

Program 3.7 will display the message in the print statement as the expression speed==110 evaluates to True.

Program 3.7
```
speed = 110
if (speed == 110):
    print ('Beware - you are driving at maximum speed!')
```

Output:
```
Beware - you are driving at maximum speed!
```

Here are more examples.

Program 3.8
```
mark = 77
if (mark >= 50):
    print ('You have passed!')
```

Output
```
You have passed!
```

Program 3.9
```
mark = 66
if (mark >=0 && mark <=100):
    print ('The mark is valid.')
```

Output:
```
The mark is valid.
```

28

▪ **if...else**

This type takes the form

```
if (expression):
    statement1    # code block
else:
    statement2    # code block
```

If expression evaluates to True, statement1 (code block) is executed; otherwise statement2 (code block) is executed. Only one of the code blocks will be executed.

Here are some examples.

Program 3.10 will execute only the second print statement as the first condition evaluates to False so control passes to the else block.

Program 3.10
```
mark = 120
if (mark >=0 && mark <=100):
    print ('The mark is valid. ')
else:
    print ('The mark is invalid. ')
```

Output
```
The mark is invalid.
```

Program 3.11 will execute only the first print statement as the first condition evaluates to True.

Program 3.11
```
speed = 100
if (speed <= 110):
    print ('Your speed is OK! ')
else:
    print ('You have committed a traffic offense! ')
```

Output
```
Your speed is OK!
```

Here are more examples.

Program 3.12
```
speed = 200
if (speed < 110):
    print ('Your speed is OK! ')
else:
    print ('You are driving recklessly! ')
```

Output
```
You are driving recklessly!
```

Program 3.13
```
mark = 77
if (mark >= 50):
    print ('Congrats - you passed the test! ')
else:
    print ('Sorry, you failed the test. ')
```

Output
```
Congrats - you passed the test!
```

Program 3.14
```
mark = 27
if (mark >= 50):
    print ('Congrats - you passed the test! ')
else:
    print ('Sorry, you failed the test. ')
```

Output
```
Sorry, you failed the test.
```

▪ if…elif…else

This type takes the form

```
if (expression1):
    statement1              # code block
elif (expression2):
    statement2
elif (expression3):
    statement3
...
else:
    statement_blockn
```

Here, if expression1 evaluates to True, statement1 is executed and the if statement *terminates*. If expression1 is False, expression2 is evaluated. If it evaluates to True, statement2 is executed and the if statement terminates. If False, the process continues. If none of the conditions is True, statement3 is executed. Again, only one of the code blocks will be executed.

Here are some examples.

Program 3.15 will execute only the second print statement as the first condition evaluates to False. Once a condition evaluates to True, the rest of conditions in the statement are not tested.

Program 3.15
```
color = 'green'
if (color == 'red'):
    print ('Stop!')
elif (color == 'green'):
    print ('Go! ')
elif (color == 'green'):
    print ('Wait!')
else:
    print ('Invalid color!')
```

Output
```
Go!
```

If you assign: color = 'purple', the above will output Invalid color!

Here are more examples.

Program 3.16
```
mark = 77
if (mark < 50):
    print ('F')
elif (mark < 60):
    print ('D')
elif (mark < 70):
```

```
    print ('C')
elif (mark < 80):
    print ('B')
else:
    print ('A')
```

Output
B

Program 3.17
```
credit_limit = 20000
customer_status = 'poor'
if (credit_limit < 20000 && customer_status = 'good'):
    print ('Approve')
elif (credit_limit < 20000 && customer_status = 'fair'):
    print ('Approve with caution')
else:
    print ('Reject')
```

Output
Reject

4.3 Loops

This control structure allows you to loop through a code block *repeatedly* until a certain condition occurs. You use this structure whenever you need to process all the items or records in a given list or application, for example, to calculate and print the pay slip of all employees in an organization, or to calculate and print the exam results of all the students in a class.

This control flow comes in several flavors:

```
1)  for
2)  for...else
3)  while
4)  while...else
5)  nested loops
```

▪ **for**

This type comes in three forms:

```
1)  for index in range (n):        # index value ranges from 0 to n-1
        statements

2)  for index in range (l, h):     # index value ranges from l to h
        statements

3)  for index in range (l, h, i):  # index value ranges from l, l+i, … hi
        statements
```

The range function specifies the number of times to loop through the statements (or code block). Note the different ways of specifying the range. The loop index controls the for loop. That means you *cannot* change its value within the loop. You can *read* or *reference* the loop index but not change/update its value.

Here are some examples.

Program 3.18 prints the value of i from 0 to 6. It starts from 0 to 6 (7-1). This is how this range function with one parameter works. Also note the use of end = ' ' in the print statement (function) to provide

31

one spacing between successive values of i on the same line. If you don't use this, each value of i will be printed on a different line.

Program 3.18
```
# illustrates for loop using the range function)
for i in range (7): # i ranges from 0 to 6 (not 7)
    print(i, end = ' ') # end = ' ' prints a blank space on the same line
```

Output
```
0 1 2 3 4 5 6
```

Program 3.19 prints the value of i from 1 to 7. If you want the index to start from 1 to 7, use this type of range function with the starting and ending value.

Program 3.19
```
# print numbers from 1 to 7
for i in range (1, 7):
    print(i, end = ' ')
```

Output
```
1 2 3 4 5 6 7
```

Program 3.20 illustrates loop index incrementation each time through the loop cycle. The last value 2 in (1, 7, 2) specifies the increment. Thus the loop index i takes the value of 1, then 3, 5 and 7.

Program 3.20
```
# print numbers from 1, 3,...to 7
for i in range (1, 7, 2): # i is incremented by 2 each time thru loop
    print(i, end = ' ')
```

Output
```
1 3 5 7
```

Program 3.21 illustrates processing all items in a list. The loop (for i in mylist) goes through all the items in mylist.

Program 3.21
```
# using for loop using a list
mylist = [1, 2, 3, 4, 5]
for i in mylist:
    print(i, end = ' ')
```

Output
```
1 2 3 4 5
```

Program 3.22 performs *elementwise* vector addition. It adds the corresponding elements of vectors x and y and stores the result in vector in z. Note the repetition/replication operator in statement z = [0] * 5 initializes all the elements of z to zero.

Program 3.22
```
# adding corresponding items in x and y and storing in z
x = [1, 2, 3, 4, 5]
y = [11, 22, 33, 44, 55]
z = [0] * 5  # this will result in [0, 0, 0, 0,0 ]
n = len(x)
for i in range(n):
    z[i] = x[i] + y[i]
print ('Sum of corresponding items in list x and y: ')
print ('z = ', z)
```

Output
```
Sum of corresponding items in list x and y:
z = [12, 24, 36, 48, 60]
```

Program 3.23 illustrates a concise way of generating (random) numbers in a list. First it imports the random function randint from the module random. Then it declares list r implicitly and fills it with 10 integer random numbers in the range [100, 999]. Note the use of for loop within the list. This is a powerful way of building list items.

Program 3.23
```
from random import randint
r = [randint(100, 999) for i in range(10)]
print ('Random numbers between 100 and 999:\n', r)
```

Sample Output
```
Random numbers between 100 and 999:
 [113, 686, 484, 134, 538, 865, 623, 791, 368, 328]
```

The for statement can also take the form

- **for...else**

This form is useful in certain situations such as when a loop terminates without a successful match in a series of comparisons.

Here is an example.

Program 3.24 generates an integer *random number* in the range 1 to 10. Then it asks you to guess the random number. If your guess is correct, it displays the message Good guess - congratulations! If your guess is wrong, it displays the message Bad guess - try again! It gives you three attempts to guess the random number correctly. If you are unsuccessful, it displays the message Sorry, your guess was wrong in all 3 attempts!

The statements

```
import random
rnd = random.randint(1, 10)
```

imports the random module and calls the randint()function to generate integer random numbers in the range (1,10).

Program 3.24
```
# illustrates the use of for...else statement
# import random number generator
import random
for i in range(1, 4):
    rnd = random.randint(1, 10)
    print ('Guess number: ', i)
    guess = int(input('Enter an integer between 1 and 10: '))
    if guess == rnd:
        print ('Good guess - congratulations!')
        print ('Generated number: {0}\tYour guess: {1}\n'.format(rnd, \
            guess))
        break
    else:
        print ('Bad guess - try again!')
        print ('Generated number: {0}\tYour guess: {1}\n'.format(rnd, \
            guess))
else:
```

```
    print ('Sorry, your guess was wrong in all {0} attempts!'.format(i))
print ('\nGuessing game over!')
```

Sample Output 1
```
Guess number:   1

Enter an integer between 1 and 10: 5
Bad guess - try again!
Generated number: 10      Your guess: 5

Guess number:   2

Enter an integer between 1 and 10: 2
Bad guess - try again!
Generated number: 6       Your guess: 2

Guess number:   3

Enter an integer between 1 and 10: 8
Bad guess - try again!
Generated number: 1       Your guess: 8
Sorry, your guess was wrong in all 3 attempts!

Guessing game over!
```

Sample Output 2
```
Guess number:   1

Enter an integer between 1 and 10: 4
Good guess - congratulations!
Generated number: 4       Your guess: 4

Guessing game over!
```

▪ Nested `for` loops

This takes the form

```
for i in range (r1, r2):
    statement1
    for (j in range (r3, r4):
        statement2
```

where i and j are loop indexes and r1 and r2 are range values for the *outer* loop, and r3 and r4 are range values for the *inner* loop.

Nesting loops means putting one loop within another loop. You can nest as many loops as you need for your application. You must however follow a simple rule: the loop indexes (i and j) must be *different* and you are *not* allowed to change their values within their scope.

Typically, the *inner* loop will execute fully for each outer loop cycle. For example, if the outer loop index ranges from 1 to m, and the inner loop index ranges from 1 to n, the inner loop will execute m *n times.

Program 3.25 illustrates nesting of two `for` loops. It uses the loops to print a multiplication table. The first `for` loop prints the column heading. The last two nested `for` loops with loop index i and j does the multiplication. The loop index i is also used to print row heading in the first column.
Program 3.25
```
# generates a multiplication table
print ('\n\t\tMultiplication Table\n')
```

34

```
# prints the top label
for i in range (1,6):    # print label
    print('\t', i, end=' ')
print ('\n')

# prints the multiplication table
for i in range (1, 5):
    print(i, end = '\t')  # i print the row label
    for j in range (1, 6):
        print ('', i*j, end = '\t')
    print ('\n')
```

Output

	1	2	3	4	5
1	1	2	3	4	5
2	2	4	6	8	10
3	3	6	9	12	15
4	4	8	12	16	20

Multiplication Table

Program 3.26 uses two nested `for` loops to print a pattern with the asterisk character (*). Note that the inner loop uses the outer loop's index i but doesn't change its value.

Program 3.26
```
# generates a pattern
for i in range (1, 6):
    print()
    for j in range (i, 6):  # range uses index i
        print ('*', end = ' ')
```

Output
```
* * * * *
* * * *
* * *
* *
*
```

Program 3.27 is similar but prints the pattern in the inverse order.

Program 3.27
```
# generates another pattern
for i in range (0, 6):
    print()
    for j in range (0, i):  # range uses index i
        print ('*', end = ' ')
```

Output
```
*
* *
* * *
* * * *
* * * * *
```

Program 3.28 illustrates several things: the `format` function, nested loops, and the tab escape sequence (\t).

Program 3.28
```
# print if product of i and j = 10
for i in range (1, 15):
    for j in range (1, 20):
        if i*j == 10:
            print ('i={0}\tj={1}\ti*j={2}'.format(i, j, i*j))
```

Output
```
i=1       j=10      i*j=10

i=2       j=5       i*j=10

i=5       j=2       i*j=10

i=10      j=1       i*j=10
```

▪ while

This takes the form

```
while (expression)
    statements
```

Here, as long as the `expression` evaluates to `True`, the `statements` will be executed repeatedly. The `while` statement will terminate only when the `expression` evaluates to `False`.

In Program 3.29 the `while` loop will execute until the condition `count < 5` becomes `False`.

Program 3.29
```
count = 0
while (count < 5): # loop thru until condition is False (count = 5)
    print (count)
    count = count + 1
```

Output
```
0
1
2
3
4
```

In Program 3.30 the `while` loop will execute until `count` reaches zero (`False`).

Program 3.30
```
count = 5
while (count):     # loop thru until condition is False (0)
    print (count)
    count = count - 1
```

Output
```
5
4
3
2
```

Program 3.31 sums (totals) a set of integers entered from the keyboard and displays the sum when the user enters the value 0. The `while` loop will execute until the user enters zero.

Program 3.31
```
# sum numbers
sum = 0
x = 1
while (x !=0): # loop until x = 0
    x = int(input('Enter number(0 to quit): '))
    sum = sum + x
print ('Sum = ', sum)
```

Output

```
Enter number(0 to quit): 7

Enter number(0 to quit): 9

Enter number(0 to quit): 15

Enter number(0 to quit): 29

Enter number(0 to quit): 0

Sum =    60
```

Program 3.32 is similar but it uses the Boolean constant `True` for the `while` expression. The user must enter a 0 to exit the loop.

Program 3.32
```
# another way to sum/total numbers

sum = 0
n = 0
while (True):
    x = int(input('Enter number (0 to quit): '))
    if x != 0:
        sum = sum + x
        n = n + 1
    else:
        break
print ('Sum of {0} numbers = {1}'.format (n, sum))
```

Sample Output

```
Enter number (0 to quit): 25

Enter number (0 to quit): 79

Enter number (0 to quit): 123

Enter number (0 to quit): 0

Sum of 3 numbers = 227
```

Program 3.33 prints the items in list x. It uses the `len()` function to get the length of the list.

Program 3.33
```
x = [5, 6, 7, 8, 9]
i = 0
while i < len(x):
    print (x[i], end = ' ')
    i = i + 1
```

Output
```
5 6 7 8 9
```

The while statement can also take the form

- **while … else**

Like the for...else, this form is also useful in certain situations, for example, when a loop completes without finding a match for an item in a list.

Program 3.34 illustrates this. Given the lists country and capital, the program asks you to enter a country name. If the country entered is in the country list, it prints its capital. Otherwise, it prints the message that the country is not in the list.

Note that the program uses two functions: len() to calculate the number of countries in the list, and lower() to convert the country name to lowercase (in case the input is in uppercase). You need to convert to one case because Python strings are case-sensitive.

Program 3.34
```
# illustrates while...else statement

country = ['malaysia', 'vietnam', 'myanmar', 'china', 'sri lanka', 'japan']
capital = ['kuala lumpur', 'hanoi', 'yangon', 'beijing', 'colombo', 'tokyo']

n = len(country)
ctry = input('Enter country: ')
ctry = ctry.lower()
i = 0
while (i < n):
    if ctry == country[i]:
        print ('Country: {0}\tCapital: {1}'.format(ctry, capital[i]))
        break
    else:
        i = i + 1
        continue  # continue the while loop
else:
    print ('{0} is not in the list'.format(ctry))
print ('Search done!')
```

Sample Output 1
```
Enter country: china
Country: china  Capital: beijing
Search done!
```

Sample Output 2
```
Enter country: usa
usa is not in the list
Search done!
```

4.4 Other Control Flows

Besides these control structures, there are others that are useful in certain situations. These are break, continue and pass.

▪ break

The break statement is useful to terminate a loop *prematurely*. You can use this statement in a for or while loop.

Here are some examples.

Program 3.35 checks if a country is in the country list x; if it is, it breaks (exits) the loop without completing it.

Program 3. 35
```
# illustrates break statement
x = ['Korea', 'Malaysia', 'Japan', 'Thailand', 'Vietnam', 'Cambodia']
for country in x:
    if (country == 'Vietnam'): # breaks the loop if condition is True
        break
    print (country)
```

Output
```
Korea
Malaysia
Japan
Thailand
```

Program 3.36 uses a for loop to check if there is an even number in list x. If there is, it skips the rest of the items in the list.

Program 3. 36
```
# finds the 1st even number in the list
x = [1, 3, 5, 7, 9, 10, 11, 13]
for i in x:
    if (i%2 == 0):      # checks if i even (0 remainder)
        break
print ('First even number is: ', i)
```

Output
```
First even number is:  10
```

Program 3.37 uses a while loop to print all numbers between 1 and 50 that are divisible by 7.

Program 3. 37
```
n = 0
while n < 50:
    n = n + 1
    if n % 7 == 0: # checks if n is divisible by 7
        print (n, 'is divisible by 7')
    else:
        continue
```

\Output
```
7 is divisible by 7

14 is divisible by 7
```

```
21 is divisible by 7

28 is divisible by 7

35 is divisible by 7

42 is divisible by 7

49 is divisible by 7
```

▪ continue

The continue statement skips the rest of the statements in a for or while loop and continues the next loop cycle without terminating the loop (unlike the break statement).

Program 3.38 checks if a number from 1 to 10 is divisible by 3. If it finds one, it continues on to find the next number.

Program 3. 38
```
# finds all the numbers divisible by 3 in a range

for i in range (1, 10):
    if (i % 3 == 0):       # i is divisible by 3
        print (i, 'is divisible by 3')
        continue  # continue the next loop cycle
    else:
        print (i, 'is not divisible by 3')
```

Output
```
1 is not divisible by 3

2 is not divisible by 3

3 is divisible by 3

4 is not divisible by 3

5 is not divisible by 3

6 is divisible by 3

7 is not divisible by 3

8 is not divisible by 3

9 is divisible by 3
```

▪ pass

The pass statement serves as a useful *placeholder*. It does nothing; it can be used for inserting code later, for example in a function or a class.

Here is an example.

Program 3.39 checks if letter g is in the string `Programmig`. If it is, it does nothing; if not, it prints that the letter is not a g.

Program 3. 39
```
for letter in 'Programmig':
    if letter == 'g':
        pass  # do nothing
    else:
        print ('Non-g letter:', letter)
```

Output

```
Non-g letter: P

Non-g letter: r

Non-g letter: o

Non-g letter: r

Non-g letter: a

Non-g letter: m

Non-g letter: m

Non-g letter: i
```

4.5 Sample Programs

Program 3.40 has several country names and their capitals and email address code. It asks the user to enter the country name and prints its capital and Internet code if the country is in the list and the message Country not list if the country is not in the list. It uses the function `lower()` to convert the input to lowercase (as the country list stores the country names in lowercase). It also uses the function `len()` to find the number of countries in the list.

Program 3.40
```
country = ['malaysia', 'vietnam', 'myanmar', 'china',
           'sri lanka', 'japan']

capital = ['kuala lumpur', 'hanoi', 'yangon', 'beijing',
           'colombo', 'tokyo']

code = ['my', 'vn', 'mm', 'cn', 'lk', 'jp']

ctry = input('\nEnter country name: ')
ctry = ctry.lower()

for i in range (len(country)):
    if ctry == country[i]:
        print ('Country:', ctry)
        print ('Capital:', capital[i])
        print ('Country:', code[i])
        break
else:
    print ('Country not list')
```

Sample run 1
```
Enter country name:vietnam
Country: vietnam
Capital:   hanoi
Country: vn
```

Sample run 2
```
Enter country name: CHINA
Country: china
Capital: beijing
Country: cn
```

Sample run 3
```
Enter country name: france
Country not list
```

Program 3.41 illustrates `for` and `while` loops and `if...elif...else` decision structure. It calculates the tax amount for different salary ranges based on a progressive taxation scheme. The `for` loop calculates the tax brackets for the different salary ranges. The `while` loop allows the user to enter salaries and get the tax amounts. It will only terminate when the user enters a -1 (or any negative integer). The `if...elif...else` determines which tax rate and tax bracket to use.

Program 3.41
```python
rate = [0.06, 0.09, 0.12, 0.15, 0.20, 0.30]
salary = [36000, 45000, 60000, 80000, 100000, 120000]
bracket = [0]*6

for i in range(len(salary)):
    bracket[i] = rate[i] * salary[i]

while (True):
    x = int(input('Enter salary: (-1 to exit): '))
    if x < 0:
        break
    if x <= salary[0]:
        tax = 0
    elif x <= salary[1]:
        tax = bracket[0] + (x-salary[0]) * rate[0]
    elif x <= salary[2]:
        tax = bracket[1] + (x-salary[1]) * rate[1]
    elif x <= salary[3]:
        tax = bracket[2] + (x-salary[2]) * rate[2]
    elif x <= salary[4]:
        tax = bracket[3] + (x-salary[3]) * rate[3]
    else:
        tax = bracket[4] + (x-salary[4]) * rate[4]
    print ('Your tax amount is: %.2f' % tax)
```

Sample run
```
Enter salary: (-1 to exit): 20000
Your tax amount is: 0.00

Enter salary: (-1 to exit): 36000
Your tax amount is: 0.00

Enter salary: (-1 to exit): 40000
Your tax amount is: 2400.00

Enter salary: (-1 to exit): 55000
Your tax amount is: 4950.00

Enter salary: (-1 to exit): 85000
```

```
Your tax amount is: 12750.00

Enter salary: (-1 to exit): 115000
Your tax amount is: 23000.00

Enter salary: (-1 to exit): 120000
Your tax amount is: 24000.00

Enter salary: (-1 to exit): 200000
Your tax amount is: 40000.00

Enter salary: (-1 to exit): -1
```

Program 3.42 uses a for loop and an if statement to get product information given its code.

Program 3.42
```
# get product info
pid = ['che', 'mil', 'but', 'yog', 'cok', 'spr', 'pep']
name = ['cheese', 'milk', 'butter', 'yogurt', 'coke', 'sprite', 'pepsi']
price = [10.50, 12.70, 12.30, 25.90, 5.90, 6.50, 6.20]

p = input('Enter product code: ')

for i in range(len(pid)):
    if p == pid[i]:
        print('id\tname\tprice')
        print ('{}\t{}\t{}'.format(p, name[i], price[i]))
        break
else:
    print ('produce not in list')
```

Sample run 1
```
Enter product code: yog
id        name       price
yog       yogurt     25.9
```

Sample run 2
```
Enter product code: ice
produce not in list
```

Program 3.43 is similar to the above but uses a dictionary. Note that it uses the key and value pair to access the items and also the method items().

Program 3.43
```
# get product info
prod = {'che': 'cheese', 'mil': 'milk', 'but': 'butter', 'yog': 'yogurt',
        'cok': 'coke', 'spr': 'sprite', 'pep': 'pepsi'}

price = [10.50, 12.70, 12.30, 25.90, 5.90, 6.50, 6.20]

print (prod)
print (price)
p = input('Enter product code: ')
i = 0

for key, value in prod.items():
    if p == key:
        print('id\tname\tprice')
        print ('{}\t{} \t{:.2f}'.format(key, value, price[i]))
        i = i + 1
        break
else:
```

```
    print ('product not in list')
```

Sample run
```
{'che': 'cheese', 'mil': 'milk', 'but': 'butter', 'yog': 'yogurt', 'cok':
'coke', 'spr': 'sprite', 'pep': 'pepsi'}
[10.5, 12.7, 12.3, 25.9, 5.9, 6.5, 6.2]

Enter product code: but
id       name     price
but      butter   10.50
```

Program 3.44 generates a list of randomly-generated seven-character passwords from a set of alphanumeric and special characters. Note that that it imports the module random and also uses the method choice() to randomly pick a character from the list.

Program 3.44
```
import random

s1 = 'abcdefghijklmnopqrstuvwxyz'
s2 = 'ABCDEFGHIJKLMNOPQRSTUVWXYZ'
s3 = '0123456789'
s4 = '!@#$%^&*(){}[]'
s = s1 + s2 + s3 + s4

print('Passwords:')

for i in range(5):
    pwd = ''
    for j in range(7):
        pwd = pwd + random.choice(s)
    print ('password', i+1, ': ', pwd)
```

Sample run
```
Passwords:
password 1 :  Bw1e]nR
password 2 :  XC7dF3R
password 3 :  %Kv*fbe
password 4 :  $F]M6lf
password 5 :  asPxNgw
```

Program 3.45 uses shuffle() method to shuffle the items in the country list randomly.

Program 3.45
```
import random
country = ['malaysia', 'vietnam', 'myanmar', 'china', 'sri lanka', 'japan']
print ('before shuffling:')
print (country)
random.shuffle(country) # shuffles the country list randomly
print ('after before shuffling:')
print (country)
```

Sample run
```
['malaysia', 'vietnam', 'myanmar', 'china', 'sri lanka', 'japan']
['china', 'sri lanka', 'japan', 'malaysia', 'vietnam', 'myanmar']
```

Program 3.46 uses the choice() method to randomly select an item from the country list.

Program 3.46
```
import random
country = ['malaysia', 'vietnam', 'myanmar', 'china', 'sri lanka', 'japan']
```

```
c = random.choice(country)
print (c)
```

```
vietnam
```

Program 3.47 generates a list of 20 integer random numbers in x in the range [100, 999]. It appends the numbers to the list one by one using a for loop.

Program 3.47
```
from random import randint
x = []
for i in range(20):
    x.append(randint(100, 999))
    print (x[i], end = ' ')
```

Sample run
```
701 856 516 734 574 787 937 705 854 663 340 543 525 179 421 350 160 753 589 558
```

Program 3.48 similar to the above but it uses a *list comprehension*. It generates a list of 20 integer random numbers in x in the range [100, 999]. Note how it uses the for loop within the list.

Program 3.48
```
from random import randint

x = [randint(100, 999) for i in range(20)]
print (x)
```
```
[481, 212, 604, 253, 496, 525, 343, 376, 317, 850, 139, 435, 459, 400, 219, 338,
705, 550, 216, 993]
```

Program 3.49 makes use of the statistics module and its methods mean, median, mode, stdev (standard deviation) and variance.

Program 3.49
```
import statistics as s  # s is a shorthand notation for statistics

x = [1, 2, 5, 3, 4, 3, 6, 7, 8, 9]
print ('Mean = {:.2f}'.format(s.mean(x)))
print ('Mode = {:.2f}'.format(s.mode(x)))
print ('Median = {:.2f}'.format(s.median(x)))
print ('Std. Dev = {:.2f}'.format(s.stdev(x)))
print ('Variance = {:.2f}'.format(s.variance(x)))
```

Output
```
Mean = 4.80
Mode = 3.00
Median = 4.50
Std. Dev = 2.66
Variance = 7.07
```

Exercise

1. Write a program that will read the name of a customer and his account balance and display the message <name>, you are a very good customer if his balance is 50,000 or more, and the message <name>, you are not a bad customer if the amount is less than 50,000.

2. Modify the program in question 2 and display the message as follows:

<name>, you are an excellent customer if the balance is greater than or equal to 100,000;
<name>, you are a good customer if the balance is greater than or equal to 50,000 but less than 100,000;
<name>, you are not a bad customer if the balance is less than 50,000.

3. Write if...else if statement that will cause the computer to beep if the user enters a number between 15 to 25.

4. What is wrong with the following statement?

```
if loan > balance
  print ('You have overdrawn. ')
else
    print ('You still have balance. ')
```

5. Rewrite the following nested if statement using a single if statement:

```
if (a > 3):
    if (b > 10):
        answer = 'OK'
```

6. Write a while loop that will go on reading integer values until the user enters a negative number.

7. Write a nested for loop where the inner loop executes five times and the outer loop executes four times.

8. Explain the difference between a while and a for loop.

9. How many times will the following loop execute?

```
i = 10
while i >= 1:
    i = i - 1
```

10. Write a program to multiply two matrices. Test your program with three sets of data.

11. Given names of students and their marks for the course Python Programming. Write a program to:

    a) Calculate their grades: 0-49 = F, 50-59 = D, 60-69 = C, 70-79 = B, 80-100 = A.
    b) Calculate the average and standard deviation.
    c) Calculate the maximum, minimum and range.

12. Write a program that will print the message Congratulations - Good guess! if the user guesses correctly the sum of points when three dices are tossed, and the message Bad guess - Try again! if the guess is wring wrong. Give the user up to 5 tries.

13. Write a program that will count the number of odd numbers in a list of integers.

14. Write a program to generate the following patterns:

(a)	(b)	(c)
*******	*******	*******
******	******	******
*****	*****	*****
****	****	****

```
***        ***      ***
**         **       **
*          *        *
```

Chapter 4

Advanced Data Types

Learning Outcomes:

After completing this chapter, the student will be able to work with the following data structures:

- *Lists*
- *Tuples*
- *Dictionaries*
- *Sets*
- *Arrays*
- *Queues*
- *Stacks*

4.1 Lists

A list in Python is a collection of items, separated by commas, and enclosed within *square* brackets ([ ]). It is similar to arrays in programming languages such as C++, C# and Java, but with one important difference. Items (elements) in a list need not be of the same data type - they can be a mixture of different data types - numbers, strings, Boolean, or even lists.

You can access the items in a list by using an *index* and/or a *slice operator* ([ ] or [:]). The index specifies the *position* of an item in the list. The *index* starts from 0 at the beginning to the end of the list, or starts with -1 at the end to the beginning of the list. The first item is indexed by 0 and the last item by -1.

The plus (+) and asterisk (*) signs in Python also double up as *concatenation* and *repetition* operators respectively. The + concatenates (joins) two lists, and the * repeats or replicates a list.

Here are some examples of lists.

The code snippet below (Program 4.1) illustrates lists. The list age has only numbers; name and pattern has only string; and others have both numbers and strings.

Program 4.1
```
name = ['Wong', 'Mary', 'Zainal']
age = [30, 27, 28]
name_age = ['Wong', 30, 'Mary', 27, 'Zainal', 28]
city_pop = ['L', 4, 'Jakarta', 8]
stud_mark = ['Ali', 66, 'Lim', 80, 'May', 88]
mixed = [12.7, 'Japan', 999, 'apple']
pattern = ['@@@$###']
```

You can display/print some or all the items of a list in several ways as shown in Program 4.2. (For convenience, we have included the output inside the code as comments.)

Program 4.2
```
print (name)            # prints all items
# Output: ['Wong', 'Mary', 'Zainal']
```

48

```
print (name[-1])          # prints last item
# Output: ['Zainal']

print (name[:-2])         # prints beginning to second
# Output: ['Wong', 'Mary']

print (name[0])           # prints 1st item (0th position]
# Output: ['Wong']

print (name[1:2])         # prints 2nd and 3rd items
# Output: ['Mary', 'Zainal']

print (name [1:])         # prints 2nd to last item
# Output: ['Mary', 'Zainal']

print (name + age)        # prints name and age
# Output: ['Wong', 'Mary', 'Zainal', 30, 27, 28]

print (age * age)         # prints age 2 times
# Output: [30, 27, 28, 30, 27, 28]

print (pattern * 3)       # prints pattern 3 times
# Output: ['@@@$###', '@@@$###', '@@@$###']

print (mixed[:])          # print all items
# Output: [12.7, 'Japan', 999, 'apple']

print (stud_mark[-1:-4])  # prints the last 4 items
# Output: ['Lim', 80, 'May', 88]
```

Items in a list can themselves be lists. A list that contains other lists is called a *nested* list.

Here are some examples of nested lists.

Program 4.3 shows lists where some items are lists. Note how the slice operator works with lists whose items are themselves lists.

Program 4.3
```
name_age = [['May', 'John', 'Wong'], [30, 28, 32]]

mixed = [1, 2, [11,12], 'a', 'b', ['aa', 'bb']]

print (name_age)
# Output: [['May', 'John', 'Wong'], [30, 28, 32]]

print (mixed)
# Output: [1, 2, [11, 12], 'a', 'b', ['aa', 'bb']]

print (name_age[0][1])  # print item 2 of the 1st item which is a list
# Output: John

print (name_age[1][2])
# Output: 32

print (name_age[-1])    # print the last item which is a list
# Output: [30, 28, 32]

print (name_age[-2][1])
# Output: John
```
Lists are *mutable* data structures, meaning, they can be updated. You can add or insert new items into a list, and delete items from a list.

4.2 Tuples

A tuple is a collection of items separated by commas and enclosed by round brackets (( )). Tuples are quite similar to lists, but with an important difference: List items and size can be changed but tuple items and size *cannot* be changed. In other words, tuples are *immutable* data structures – they cannot be updated. Tuples can be thought of as *read-only* lists.

Here are some examples of tuples.

Program 4.4 illustrates tuples with string and number items. Like lists, tuple items can also take on different data types.

Program 4.4
```
country = ('Malaysia', 'Indonesia', 'Thailand')
capital = ('KL', 'Jakarta' 'Bangkok')
color = ('red', 'green', 'yellow')
name_id = ('John', '1234567', 'Susan', '3456789')
odd = (1, 3, 5, 7, 9)
even = (0, 2, 4, 6, 8)
```

Like lists, you can display/print some or all the items in a tuple in several ways as in Program 4.5.

Program 4.5
```
print (country)          # prints all items
# Output: ('Malaysia', 'Indonesia', 'Thailand')

print (capital[0])       # prints 1st item
# Output: ('KL')

print (colour[1:2])      # prints 2nd and 3rd items
# Output: ('green', 'yellow')

print (name_id[2:])      # prints from 3rd to last item
# Output: ('Susan', '3456789')

print (odd[:])           # prints all items
# Output: (1, 3, 5, 7, 9)

print (odd[1:3])         # prints 2nd to 4th item
# Output: (3, 5, 7)

print (even[-1])         # prints last item
# Output: (8)

print (even + odd)       # prints even and odd items
# Output: (0, 2, 4, 6, 8, 1, 3, 5, 7, 9)
```

4.3 Dictionaries

A dictionary is a kind of *hash table*. It is a collection of *paired* items in the form of *key: value*. Dictionaries are enclosed within a pair of braces/curly brackets ({ }). Like lists and tuples, dictionary items can be accessed using square brackets ([ ]) and indexes.

Dictionaries are unordered, so the concept of order doesn't arise. So it is not correct to say that the items are "out of order".

Here are some examples of dictionaries.

Program 4.6 has several dictionaries including an empty one. You can use methods like keys() and values() with dictionaries.

Program 4.6
```
empty = {}
emp = {'id': 111, 'name': 'john', 'job': 'programmer'}
stud = {'id': 123, 'name': 'susan', 'mark': 77}
item = {'code': 'ip7', 'price': 1000, 'brand': 'apple'}
country = {'name': 'malaysia', 'pop': 33}

print (emp)            # prints the entire dictionary
# Output: {'id': 111, 'name': 'john', 'job': 'programmer'}

print (stud.keys())    # prints only the keys
# Output: {'id', 'name', 'mark'}

print (stud.values())  # prints only the values
# Output: {123, 'susan', 77}

print (empty)  # no items
# Output: {}

print (country)
# Output: {'name': 'malaysia', 'pop': 33}
```

The table below give several dictionary operators and methods.

Dictionary Operators

Operator/Methods	Explanation
len(d)	Returns the number of (key, value) pairs.
del d[k]	Deletes the key k together with its value.
k in d	True, if key k exists in dictionary d.
k not in d	True, if key k doesn't exist in dictionary d.
clear()	Clears all the dictionary items, but dictionary itself is not deleted
update()	*merge* two dictionaries

Here are some examples.

Program 4.7 illustrates the clear method.

Program 4.7
```
color.clear()  # clear color
print (color)
# Output: set()
```

Program 4.8 illustrates the update method. It merges the dictionaries country and more.

Program 4.8
```
country = {'name': 'malaysia', 'pop': 33000000}
more = {'area': 330803, 'states': 13}

country.update(more)   # merge country and more
print (country)
# Output: {'name': 'malaysia', 'pop': 33000000, 'area': 330803,
# 'states': 13}
```

Program 4.9 illustrates the `in` method - it tests if `green` is in the dictionary `color`.

Program 4.9
```
color = {'red', 'green', 'yellow'}
if 'green' in color:
    print (True)
else:
    print (False)

color_copy = color.copy()       # make a copy of color
print (color_copy)

# Output: {'red', 'yellow', 'green'}
```

You can also use the in operator to iterate through a dictionary as in Program 4.10.

Program 4.10
```
country = {'name': 'malaysia', 'pop': 33000000, 'area': 330803, 'states': 13}

for key in country:
    print (key)

# Output:
        name
        pop
        area
        states
```

4.4 Sets

The set data type is similar to that used in mathematics. A set is a collection of zero or more items (members). Set functions (methods) include finding how many items are in a set, testing if an item is in the set, testing if a set is a subset of another set, taking the union, intersection or difference of two sets.

The table below gives the set functions/methods.

Method	Equivalent to	Description
len(s)		Number of elements in set s (cardinality)
x in s		Test x for membership in s
x not in s		Test x for non-membership in s
s.issubset(t)	s <= t	Test whether every element in s is in t
s.issuperset(t)	s >= t	Test whether every element in t is in s
s.union(t)	s | t	New set with elements from both s and t
s.intersection(t)	s & t	New set with elements common to both s and t
s.difference(t)	s - t	New set with elements in s but not in t
s.symmetric_difference(t)	s ^ t	New set with elements in either s or t but not both
s.copy()		New set with a shallow copy of s
s.update(t)	s |= t	Return set s with elements added from t
s.intersection_update(t)	s &= t	Return set s keeping only elements also found in t
s.difference_update(t)	s -= t	Return set s after removing elements found in t
s.symmetric_difference_update(t)	s ^= t	Return set s with elements from s or t but not both
s.add(x)		Add element x to set s
s.remove(x)		Remove x from set s; raises KeyError if not present
s.discard(x)		Removes x from set s if present

s.pop()		Remove and return an arbitrary element from s; raises KeyError if empty
s.clear()		Remove all elements from set s

Here are some examples of sets.

Program 4.11 illustrates several set methods: set, update, remove, and add.

Program 4.11
```
v = set(['a', 'e', 'i', 'o', 'u'])
v2 = set (['a', 'e'])
e = set([2, 4, 6, 8, 'e', 'u'])
print (len(v))
print ('x' in v)
print ('y' not in v)
print (v | e)      # union
print (v-e)        # difference
print (v & e)      # intersection
print (v2 <= v)
print (v < v2)

s = set([99])
v.update(s)
print (v)
v.remove(99)
print (v)
v.add(77)
print (v)
```

Output
```
5
False
True
{'e', 2, 4, 6, 8, 'u', 'o', 'a', 'i'}
{'o', 'a', 'i'}
{'e', 'u'}
True
False
{'e', 99, 'u', 'o', 'a', 'i'}
{'e', 'u', 'o', 'a', 'i'}
{'e', 'u', 77, 'o', 'a', 'i'}
```

4.5 Arrays

We can implement arrays in several ways: using lists, using array imported from the module array, or using array imported from the module numpy. (Numpy stands for number processing in Python).

- **Using Lists**

A list can be used as an array.

Here are some examples.

Program 4.12 has an array of items which themselves are lists. Note the use of double pair of brackets [ ] [ ] for indexes: the first index refers to the item in list x while the second index refers to the list item referenced by the first index. The program sums (adds) all the items in list x. It also uses the len () function to get the size of the lists.

Program 4.12
```
x = [[1, 2, 3, 4], [5, 6], [7, 8, 9]]
sum = 0
for i in range(len(x)):
    for j in range(len(x[i])):
        sum += x[i][j]
print('Sum = ', sum)
```

Output
```
Sum = 45
```

Program 4.12 computes the sum and average of all the items in list a.

Program 4.12
```
sum = 0
n = 0
a = [ [1, 2, 3], [4, 5, 6], [7, 8, 9] ]

for i in range(len(a)):
    for j in range(len(a[i])):
        n += 1
        sum += a[i][j]
        print (a[i][j], end = ' ')
    print ()

print ('Sum =', sum)
print ('Average =', round(sum/n, 2))
```

Output
```
1 2 3
4 5 6
7 8 9
Sum = 45
Average = 5.0
```

▪ Using Array Type

Unlike lists which store *heterogeneous* data, arrays store *homogeneous* data. All the items of an array are the same data type - int, float, etc. Because array items are of the same data type, processing arrays is more efficient than processing lists.

Array is not a built-in data type in Python, so you need to import the array class from the array module as follows:

```
from array import array
```

Once you have imported the array class, you can declare and use arrays. Array declaration takes the form

```
variable = array (typecode, [initializer])
```

where typecode indicates the data type (int, float, etc.) and initializer is the list of items.

The type codes and their length (in bytes) for arrays are as follows:

Type code	Represents	No. of bytes
'b'	Signed integer	1
'B'	Unsigned integer	1
'c'	Character	1
'u'	Unicode	2
'h'	Signed integer	2
'H'	Unsigned integer	2
'i'	Signed integer	2
'I'	Unsigned integer	2
'w'	Unicode character	4
'l'	Signed integer	4
'L'	Unsigned integer	4
'f'	Floating point	4
'd'	Floating point	8

Here is an example of an integer array declaration.

```
myarray = array ('i', [1, 2, 3, 4, 5])  # i specifies integer type
```

The table below gives a list of methods available for arrays.

Function/Method	Description
a.append(x)	Append a value (to the array)
a.insert(i, x)	Insert a value before item position i
a.remove(x)	Remove any array element
a.extend(y)	Extend the array with y
a.pop()	Remove the last element
a.reverse()	Reverse the array
a.tolist()	Convert array to list
a.count(x)	Count the number of occurrences of x
a.index(x)	Return the smallest i such that i is the index of the first occurrence of x
a.tofile(f)	Write all items to the file object f
a.tounicode()	Convert a (must be of type 'u') to Unicode string.

Program 4.14 illustrates some of the array methods - insert, remove, pop, reverse, etc. The type code i specifies that the array is of type int.

Program 4.14
```
# import array module
from array import array

ary = array ('i', [11, 22, 33, 44, 55]) # i specifies integer array
print (ary)

ary.append(66)          # append 66 to ary
print (ary)

ary.insert(0, 77)       # insert 77 at position 0
print (ary)

ary.remove(33)          # remove 33 from ary
print (ary)

ary.pop()               # pop the last item in ary
print (ary)

ary.reverse()           # reverse the ary
print (ary)
```

```
ary2 = [1, 2, 3, 22]
ary.extend(ary2)        # extend ary with ary2
print (ary)

alist = ary.tolist()   # convert ary to list
print (alist)
```

Output
```
array('i', [11, 22, 33, 44, 55])
array('i', [11, 22, 33, 44, 55, 66])
array('i', [77, 11, 22, 33, 44, 55, 66])
array('i', [77, 11, 22, 44, 55, 66])
array('i', [77, 11, 22, 44, 55])
array('i', [55, 44, 22, 11, 77])
array('i', [55, 44, 22, 11, 77, 1, 2, 3, 22])
[55, 44, 22, 11, 77, 1, 2, 3, 22]
```

Program 4.15 illustrates floating point arrays. The type code f specifies that the array is of type float.

Program 4.15
```
from array import array
sum = 0.0
a = array('f', [1.1, 2.2, 3.3, 4.4, 5.5])   # f specifies float array
n = len(a)   # get length of array a

for item in a:
    sum += item

avg = sum/n
print ('Sum =', round(sum, 2))
print ('Average =', round(avg, 2))
```

Output
```
Sum = 16.5
Average = 3.3
```

Program 4.16 illustrates appending two arrays (x and y) and storing it in another array (z).

Program 4.16
```
# import array module
from array import array

x = array ('i', [1, 2, 3, 4, 5])
y = array ('i', [11, 22, 33, 44, 55])
n = len(x)
z = array ('i', [])
for i in range (0, n):
    z.append(x[i] + y[i])
print ('x =', x)
print ('y =', y)
print ('z =', z)
```

Output
```
x = array('i', [1, 2, 3, 4, 5])
y = array('i', [11, 22, 33, 44, 55])
z = array('i', [12, 24, 36, 48, 60])
```

Program 4.17 illustrates adding arrays x and y elementwise and storing the result in array z.

Program 4.17
```
# add 2 lists

x = [1, 2, 3, 4, 5]
y = [11, 22, 33, 44, 55]
n = len(x)
z = [0 for i in range (n)]
for i in range (n):
    z[i] = x[i] + y[i]
print ('x =', x)
print ('y =', y)
print ('z =', z)

# simpler way using list comprehension
print ('\nUsing list comprehension:')
z = [x[i] + y[i] for i in range (n)]
print (z)
```

Output
```
x = [1, 2, 3, 4, 5]
y = [11, 22, 33, 44, 55]
z = [12, 24, 36, 48, 60]

Using list comprehension:
[12, 24, 36, 48, 60]
```

Program 4.18 computes the total and average prices.

Program 4.18
```
# import array
from array import array

price = array ('f', [1.00, 2.50, 3.70, 4.20, 5.60])
n = len(price)
total = 0.0
for i in range (0, n):
    total += price[i]
print ('Total price =', round(total, 2))
print ('Average price =', round(total/n, 2))
```

Output
```
Total price = 17.0
Average price = 3.4
```

▪ Using Numpy

Numpy is an external module, created especially for performing numerical computations using arrays.

To use this module, you need to import as follows:

```
import numpy as np
```

Once imported, you can use the numpy object np in your code.

In Python, array dimensions are called *axes*. The number of axes is called *rank*.

Numpy's array class is called ndarray. It is also known by the alias array.

The attributes of ndarray object are as follows:

57

ndarray.ndim	Number of dimensions (axes) of the array (referred to as *rank*.)
ndarray.shape	Dimensions of the array, a tuple of integers indicating the size of the array in each dimension. For an array with n rows and m columns, the shape will be (n, m). The length of the shape tuple is the rank or number of dimensions (ndim)
ndarray.size	Total number of elements in the array, equal to the product of the elements of shape.
ndarray.dtype	Object describing the type of elements in the array. You can create/specify dtype's using Python's standard types. NumPy also provides its own data types like numpy.int16, numpy.int32 and numpy.float64.
ndarray.itemsize	Size (in bytes) of each array element; this is equivalent to ndarray.dtype.itemsize.
ndarray.data	Buffer containing actual array elements.

Creating Arrays

You can create Numpy arrays from Python lists and tuples using the array object np and the array functions/methods. The data type of the elements in the sequence determines the data type of the array.

Here are some examples.

```
a = np.array([11, 22, 33, 44])   # integer array

b = np.array([1.1, 2.2, 3.3])    # float array

c = np.array([(1, 2, 3), (4, 5, 6)])
```

You can also specify the data type explicitly as follows:

```
c = np.array( [ [1.1, 2.2], [3.3, 4.4] ], dtype = float)
```

Numpy comes with several methods/functions for creating arrays with initial *placeholder* contents.

The zeros function creates an array of zeros; the ones function creates an array of ones; and the empty function creates an array with random contents. By default, the dtype of the created array is float64.

```
a = np.zeros((3,4))
a = np.ones((2,3,4), dtype=np.int16)    # specifies dtype
a = np.empty((2,3))                     # contents will be random
```

To create a sequence of numbers, Numpy provides arange method similar to range that returns arrays instead of lists.

```
a = np.arange(10, 30, 5)

a = np.arange(0.4, 2.7, 0.3)
```

Array Operations

You can perform array operations using numpy methods.

Here are some examples.

Program 4.19 illustrates matrix addition, subtraction, multiplication of every element by a scalar, etc.

Program 4.19

```
import numpy as np
a = np.array([25, 30, 48, 50])
b = np.arange(4)
print ('a = \n', a)
print ('b = \n', b)

c = a - b  # array subtraction
print ('c = \n', c)

d = a + b  # array addition
print ('d = \n', d)

e = b ** 2  # exponentiation of every element
print ('e = \n', e)

f = a * 2  # multiplication of every element
print ('f = \n', f)
```

Output

```
a =
 [25 30 48 50]
b =
 [0 1 2 3]
c =
 [25 29 46 47]
d =
 [25 31 50 53]
e =
 [0 1 4 9]
f =
 [ 50  60  96 100]
```

The product operator * applied to matrices operates *elementwise*. To obtain the elementwise product of two matrices, you can use the dot method.

Program 4.20 illustrates many things: elementwise multiplication using the product operator *, matrix product by using the dot() method, the sum() method to add all the elements in array f, min() and max() methods to find the maximum and minimum. It also uses the zeros() method to create a matrix of zeros, and a random() method to generate a matrix of random numbers.

Program 4.20

```
import numpy as np
a = np.array( [[1,2],[1,5]] )
b = np.array( [[2,0],[3,4]] )
c = a + b                         # elementwise addition
d = a * b                         # elementwise product
e1 = a.dot(b)                     # matrix product
e2 = np.dot(a, b)                 # same as above
print ('a = \n', a)
print ('b = \n', b)
print ('c = \n', c)
print ('d = \n', d)
print ('e1 = \n', e1)
print ('e2 = \n', e2)

print (a.sum())  # sum all elements of a
print (a.sum(axis = 0)) # sum column elements

f = np.array( [1,2,3,4,5,6,7] )
print ('sum = ', f.sum())  # sum all the elements of f
print ('min = ', f.min())  # get the minimum
```

```
print ('max = ', f.max())  # get the maximum

x = np.ones((2,3), dtype=int)   # array of 1s
y = np.zeros((2,3), dtype=int)  # array of 0s
print ('x = \n', x)
print ('y = \n', y)

# this is numpy's random function
z = np.random.random((2,3))   # create 2x3 array of random numbers
print ('z = \n', z)
```

Output
```
a =
 [[1 2]
  [1 5]]
b =
 [[2 0]
  [3 4]]
c =
 [[3 2]
  [4 9]]
d =
 [[ 2  0]
  [ 3 20]]
e1 =
 [[ 8  8]
  [17 20]]
e2 =
 [[ 8  8]
  [17 20]]
9
[2 7]
sum =  28
min =  1
max =  7
x =
 [[1 1 1]
  [1 1 1]]
y =
 [[0 0 0]
  [0 0 0]]
z =
 [[ 0.14614219  0.38845125  0.2152552 ]
  [ 0.84913611  0.10262237  0.97193986]]
```

Linear Algebra

With Numpy you can also perform matrix operations like taking the transpose or inverse of a matrix, matrix multiplication, and solving linear equations.

Program 4.21 illustrates taking the transpose and inverse of a matrix, identity matrix, and matrix multiplication.

Program 4.21
```
import numpy as np
a = np.array([[1.0, 2.0], [3.0, 4.0]])
print('a = \n', a)

at = a.transpose()
print ('a transpose = \n', at)

ai = np.linalg.inv(a)
print ('a inverse = \n', ai)
```

```
e = np.eye(3)          # unit 3x3 id matrix
print ('sum of diagonal elements =', np.trace(e))

y = np.array([[0.0, -1.0], [1.0, 2.0]])
z = np.dot (y, y) # matrix product
print ('y = \n', y)
print ('y.y = \n', z)
```

Output
```
a =
 [[ 1.   2.]
 [ 3.   4.]]
a transpose =
 [[ 1.   3.]
 [ 2.   4.]]
a inverse =
 [[-2.    1. ]
 [ 1.5 -0.5]]
sum of diagonal elements = 3.0
y =
 [[ 0.  -1.]
 [ 1.   2.]]
y.y =
 [[-1.  -2.]
 [ 2.   3.]]
```

Program 4.22 illustrates solving a set of linear equations of the form ax = b where a is the coefficient matrix, x is vector of variables, and b is a vector of constants.

Program 4.22
```
import numpy as np
# solving equations: 3x + y = 9 and x + 2y = 8:
# ax = b
a = np.array([[3,1], [1,2]]) # a coef. matrix
b = np.array([9,8])          # b vector
x = np.linalg.solve(a, b)    # result vector
print ('Solving 2 equations: ', x)

# Solving equations: 3x + y -z = 5, x + 2y + 5z = 8, -2x + 4y + 7z = 12
a2 = np.array([[3, 1, -1], [1, 2, 5], [-2, 8, 7]])
b2 = np.array([5, 8, 12])
x2 = np.linalg.solve(a2, b2)
print ('Solving 3 equations', x2)
```

Output
```
Solving 2 equations:  [ 2.   3.]
Solving 3 equations [ 1.55140187  1.1682243   0.82242991]
```

Program 4.23 illustrates other features such as dimension, data type, and size.

Program 4.23
```
import numpy as np
a = np.arange(15).reshape(3, 5)
print ('array a:\n', a)
print ('no. of dimensions:', a.ndim)
print ('data type:', a.dtype)
print ('item size: ', a.itemsize)
print ('array size:', a.size)
b = np.array([6, 7, 8])
print ('array b:\n', b)
```
Output
```
array a:
```

61

```
[[ 0  1  2  3  4]
 [ 5  6  7  8  9]
 [10 11 12 13 14]]
no. of dimensions: 2
data type: int32
item size:   4
array size: 15
array b:
 [6 7 8]
```

Printing Arrays

Printing arrays in Numpy is similar way to using nested lists but with the following layout:

- The last axis is printed from left to right
- The second-to-last is printed from top to bottom
- The rest are also printed from top to bottom, with each slice separated from the next by an empty line.

Program 4.24 illustrates printing one-, two- and three-dimensional arrays.

Program 4.24
```
import numpy as np

a = np.arange(6)             # 1d array
print('\nArray a:\n', a)

b = np.arange(12).reshape(4,3)    # 2d array
print('\nArray b:\n', b)

c = np.arange(24).reshape(2,3,4)  # 3d array
print('\nArray c:\n', c)
```

Output
```
Array a:
 [0 1 2 3 4 5]

Array b:
 [[ 0  1  2]
 [ 3  4  5]
 [ 6  7  8]
 [ 9 10 11]]

Array c:
 [[[ 0  1  2  3]
  [ 4  5  6  7]
  [ 8  9 10 11]]

 [[12 13 14 15]
  [16 17 18 19]
  [20 21 22 23]]]
```

Exercise

1. Explain the difference between a list and a tuple. Give two examples where you might use each of these data structures.

2. Explain the difference between a list and a dictionary. Give two examples where you might use each of these data structures.

3. Explain the difference between a tuple and a dictionary. Give two examples where you might use each of these data structures.

4. Which data type (list, tuple or dictionary) will you use for each of the following tasks?

   (a) Performing calculations on a set of numbers
   (b) Performing operations on a set of strings
   (c) Creating a hash table
   (d) Storing telephone numbers of contacts
   (e) Storing the colors in a rainbow.

5. Given list x = [1, 2, 3, 4, 5]. Write code to perform the following tasks:

   (a) Add 10 to each item and store the result in y
   (b) Multiply each item by 7 and store the result in z
   (c) Append the list a = [20, 30, 40]
   (d) Remove item with value 30
   (e) Replace all items with zeros.

6. Given tuple color = ('violet', 'indigo', 'blue', 'green', 'yellow', 'red', 'orange'). Write code to perform the following tasks:

   (a) Print all the items
   (b) Print all items from 'blue' to 'orange'
   (c) Print the last item
   (d) Print all the items in the reverse order
   (e) Print all the items from 'indigo to 'yellow'.

7. Given dictionary prod = {'iPhone': 1200, 'laptop': 2500, 'desktop': 2900}, perform the following tasks:

   (a) Print all the items
   (b) Print all the keys
   (c) Print the key desktop and its value
   (d) Add the pairs 'GPU': 15000 and 'Mainframe':50000
   (e) Remove 'Mainframe' and its value

8. Given arrays x = [1, 3, 5, 7, 9], y = [2, 4, 6, 8, 10], perform the following, tasks:

   (a) Add x and y and store the result in z
   (b) Multiply x and y elementwise and store the result in v
   (c) Multiply each element of x by -7 and store the result in w
   (d) Replace all items in y with zeros.

9. Given a list of n=10 countries and their capitals, write a program to display the capital given the country name if the country is in the list or the message "Country not in list" if the country is not in the list.

10. Give two matrices, perform the following tasks:

$$x = \begin{matrix} 2 & -3 & 5 \\ 1 & 9 & 4 \\ 3 & -1 & 7 \end{matrix} \qquad y = \begin{matrix} -5 & 1 & 0 \\ 3 & 6 & 2 \\ 1 & 3 & 8 \end{matrix}$$

   (a) Multiply x and y and store the result in z
   (b) Transpose x and store it in v
   (c) Take the inverse of x and store in w
   (d) Find the determinant of x

11. Solve the following linear equations:

$$x - 3y + 2z = 4$$
$$2x + 4y - z = 3$$
$$3x - y + 5z = -5$$

12. Given four students and their marks in three courses as follows, perform the following tasks:

x = ['joe', [55, 77, 99], 'sam', [45, 66, 88], 'sally', [60, 80, 90], 'may', [45, 70, 85]]

   (a) Print in one line each student's name and marks
   (b) Calculate each student's name, total and average mark

13. Given a collection n=10 books with their reference numbers and titles. Write a program using the dictionary data structure to perform the following tasks:

   (a) List the entire collection
   (b) Given a reference number, display its title
   (c) Append two books with their references
   (d) Delete a book given its reference

Chapter 5

Advanced Input / Output

Learning Outcomes:

After completing this chapter, the student will be able to

- *Read input data from the keyboard.*
- *Send output to the monitor.*
- *Format output.*
- *Use escape sequences.*
- *Read input data from text files.*
- *Send output to text files.*
- *Send output to printers.*

Computer programs typically read input data, process the data, and generate output (results). Input data can come from the keyboard, or from text files (or databases) stored in a hard disk. Output can be sent to the monitor, printer, or text files.

In this chapter, you will learn how to read data from the keyboard (or console) and text files into a program, and how to send output from a program to the monitor (or console), text file, or printer.

5.1 Reading Input Data from Keyboard

Reading data from the keyboard takes the form

```
variable = input('prompt: ' )
```

where prompt prompts the use to enter a value and variable stores the value the user enters.

Program 5.1 illustrates input from keyboard (and also output to the monitor). The prompt and labels are enclosed between a pair of single quote ('). You can also use the double quote (") for both prompts and labels (but you must use them in a consistent manner - not mix the quotes).

Program 5.1
```
# read a string
s = input('Enter a string: ')

# read an integer
inum = input('Enter an integer: ')

# read a number with a decimal point
dnum = input('Enter a number with a decimal point: ')

# reads a Boolean value
b = input('Enter a Boolean value: ')

print ('\nString: ', s) # the escape sequence \n skip to next line
print ('Integer number: ', inum)
print ('Decimal number: ', dnum)
print ('Boolean value: ', b)
```
Sample interaction

```
Enter a string: do to others as you would have others do to you

Enter an integer: 567

Enter a number with a decimal point: 22.718

Enter a Boolean value: True


String:  do to others as you would have others do to you
Integer number:   567
Decimal number:   22.718
Boolean value:    True
```

Python treats all input data as *strings*. In some cases it automatically converts to the desired data type as in the above example. It is however advisable to *explicitly* convert the string input to the desired data type using appropriate conversion functions.

To convert string input data to other data types, you can use the following statement:

```
variable = <converter>(input('prompt: '))
```

where the <converter> function converts the input to data type int, float, bool, etc.

Program 5.2 illustrates this. The first input (prod) is a string, so it doesn't to be converted. The second input (price) is float type, so after reading the input it must be converted to type float. The third input is an integer, so it must be converted to type int.

The last two statements illustrate nested functions. The *inner* function input reads the input from the keyboard, and the *outer* functions float and int convert the data to the desired data type.

Program 5.2
```
# enter a string
prod = input('Enter product name: ')
# enter a number with decimal places
price = float(input('Enter price: '))    # convert to float
# enter an integer
qty = int(input('Enter quantity: '))     # convert to integer
```

Sample interaction
```
Enter product name: Pendrive

Enter price: 25.70

Enter quantity: 2
```

Here is another example using the Boolean converter bool.

Program 5.3
```
# read a string
s = input('Enter a string: ')

# read and convert to an integer
inum = int(input('Enter an integer: ')) # note 2 open and close

# read and convert to a float
dnum = float(input('Enter a number with a decimal point: '))

# read and convert to a boolean value
b = bool(input("Enter a boolean value: '))
```

66

```
print ('\nString: ', s)    # \n skip to next line before printing
print ('Integer number: ', inum)
print ('Decimal number: ', dnum)
print ('Boolean value: ', b)
```

Sample interaction
```
Enter a string: Python is a great language

Enter an integer: 567

Enter a number with a decimal point: 23.75

Enter a boolean value: True

String:  Python is a great language
Integer number:  567
Decimal number:  23.75
Boolean value:  True
```

5.2 Sending Output to Monitor

To send output (results) to the monitor, you use the print function.

Output must be presented neatly. To help you do that, Python provides several *escape sequences* and *formatting* functions.

Escape Sequences

Escape sequences are special (non-printable) characters that have specific meaning. You can use them in the print statement/function. For example, you can use the escape sequence \n to generate a linefeed (new line), \t to generate a tab, \f to generate a form feed, and \a to beep a sound.

The table below gives the list of escape sequences.

Escape Sequence	Meaning
\newline	Back slash and newline ignored
\\	Backslash
\'	Single quote
\"	Double quote
\a	Bell
\b	Backspace
\f	Formfeed
\n	Linefeed
\r	Carriage Return
\t	Horizontal Tab
\v	Vertical Tab
\ooo	Character with octal value ooo
\xhh	Character with hex value hh
\uxxxx	Character with 16-bit hex value XXXX
\Uxxxx	Character with 32-bit hex value XXXXXXXX

Note:

1) Unless an r or R (r/R stands for *raw data*) prefix is present, escape sequences in strings are interpreted as in the table. All unrecognized escape sequences are left in the string unchanged (i.e., the backslash is left in the string).

2) When an r/R prefix is present, the character following a backslash is included in the string without change, and all backslashes are left in the string. For example, the string literal r'n' consists of two characters: a backslash and the lowercase 'n'.

3) When an r/R prefix is used in conjunction with a u/U prefix, then the uxxxx and Uxxxxxxxx escape sequences are processed while all other backslashes are left in the string.

Programs 5.4 and 5.5 illustrate escape sequences. It prints the output on new lines using the escape sequence (\n).

Program 5.4
```
# illustrates linefeed (\n)
print ('This is Line 1\nThis is Line 2\nThis is Line 3')
```

Output
```
This is Line 1
This is Line 2
This is Line 3
```

Program 5.5
```
# also illustrates linefeed (\n)
name = 'Johnson'
mark = 85
grade = 'A'
print ('Name:', name, '\nMark:', mark, '\nGrade:', grade)
```

Output
```
Name: Johnson
Mark: 85
Grade: A
```

Programs 5.6 prints the output using the tab escape sequence (\t).

Program 5.6
```
# illustrates tab (\t)
name = 'Johnson'
mark = 85
grade = 'A'
print ('Name:', name, '\t\tMark:', mark, '\tGrade:', grade)
```

Output
```
Name: Johnson          Mark: 85          Grade: A
```

Program 5.7 prints the output using both new line and tab escape sequences.

Program 5.7
```
# illustrates linefeed (\n) and tab (\t)
print ('This is Line 1\n\tThis is Line 2\n\t\tThis is Line 3')
```

Output
```
This is Line 1
        This is Line 2
                This is Line 3
```

Program 5.8 prints the output using several escape sequences: new line (\n), audible bell (\a), tab (\t), Unicode (\u), and page or formfeed (\f).

Program 5.8

```
# illustrates several escape sequences
print ('\nSkip a line, then print this.')
print ('Print this, then skip a line.\n')
print ('\aFatal error!')
print ('Skip 2 lines after this.\n\n')
print ('Name\tTelephone\tEmail')
print ('\nFirst Line\n\tSecond Line\n\t\tThird Line')
print ('\uABCD')
print ('\f[New page.]')   # skip to next page and print
# to save space, no formfeed is generated in the output!
```

Output

```
Skip a line, then print this.
Print this, then skip a line.

Fatal error!
Skip 2 lines after this.


Name    Telephone       Email

First Line
        Second Line
                Third Line
□

[New page.]
```

5.3 Formatting Output

Python provides several formatting features to help you format your output the way you want. For example, you can print numbers with a specified number of decimal places, print a string left-, center- or right- justified.

The print statement/function takes several forms:

```
1) print (control string, variable, control string, variable, …)
   # The control string items can be in any order

2) print (control string % variables)

3) print (control string.format(variables))
   # This form uses the format function
```

Note:
- The control string must be enclosed between a pair of single (') or double (' ') apostrophes.
- It can include escape sequences (e.g. \n and \t).
- It can include formatting characters (e.g. %s, %d and %f) where %s is for formatting strings, %d is for formatting integers and %f is for formatting floating point numbers (i.e. numbers with decimal points).
- It can specify column widths (e.g. %3d – print the integer in 3 columns; %5s – print the string in 5 columns; %7.2f – print the floating point number in 7 columns with 2 decimal places).
- It can include placeholders { } for variables. The placeholders can be empty { } or numbered {0} {1} {2}... It can also contain formatting characters ({:5d} – print integer in 5 columns, {:7.2f} – print

floating point number in 7 columns with 2 decimal places, {:<20} – left-justify string in 20 columns, {:>20} – right-justify string in 20 columns, {:^20} – centre-justify string in 20 columns).
* The format function in the last form (3) is prefixed with a dot (.) operator.

We will illustrate all these forms by way of examples.

Program 5.9 uses format (2).

Program 5.9
```
age = 25
pay = 3500.80
name = 'sally'
print ('name: %s, age: %d, pay: %.2f' %(name, age, pay))
print ('name: %10s, age: %7d, pay: %9.2f' %(name, age, pay))
```

Output
```
name: sally, age: 25, pay: 3500.80
name:      sally, age:      25, pay:    3500.80
```

Program 5.10 uses formats (1), (2) and (3).

Program 5.10
```
age = 25
pay = 3500.80
name = 'sally'

print()

# format (1)
print ('name:', name, 'age:', age, 'pay:', pay)
print ('name:', name, '\tage:', age, '\tpay:', pay)

print()

# format (2)
print ('name: %s age: %d  pay: %f' %(name, age, pay))
print ('name: %s age: %2d  pay: %6.2f' %(name, age, pay))

print()

# format (3)
print ('name: {}\tage: {}\t\tpay: {}'.format(name, age, pay))
print ('name: {:7s}\tage: {:2d}\t\tpay: {:7.2f}'.format(name, age, pay))
```

Output
```
name: sally age: 25 pay: 3500.8
name: sally     age: 25             pay: 3500.8

name: sally age: 25  pay: 3500.800000
name: sally age: 25  pay: 3500.80

name: sally     age: 25             pay: 3500.8
name: sally     age: 25             pay: 3500.80
```

Program 5.11 also uses formats (1), (2) and (3).

Program 5.11
```
age = 25
pay = 3500.80
name = 'sally'
```

```
print()
print ('name:', name, 'age:', age, 'pay:', pay)
print ('name:', name, '\tage:', age, '\tpay:', pay)
print ('name:', name, '\nage:', age, '\npay:', pay)
print()

print ('name: %s age: %2d  pay: %6.2f' %(name, age, pay))
print ('name: %s\tage: %d\tpay: %f' %(name, age, pay))
print ('\nname: %s\nage: %2d\npay: %6.2f' %(name, age, pay))
print()
print ('name: {}\tage: {}\t\tpay: {}'.format(name, age, pay))
print ('name: {:7s}\tage: {:2d}\t\tpay: {:7.2f}'.format(name, age, pay))
print ('\nname: {:7s}\nage: {:2d}\npay: {:7.2f}'.format(name, age, pay))
```

Output
```
name: sally age: 25 pay: 3500.8
name: sally     age: 25         pay: 3500.8
name: sally
age: 25
pay: 3500.8

name: sally age: 25  pay: 3500.80
name: sally     age: 25 pay: 3500.800000

name: sally
age: 25
pay: 3500.80

name: sally     age: 25         pay: 3500.8
name: sally     age: 25         pay: 3500.80

name: sally
age: 25
pay: 3500.80
```

Program 5.12 reads a line of input data for two fields separated by comma (,). Then it splits the line to extract the two fields, and uses the format function to display the output. The placeholders {0} and {1} tell that country should be displayed first, and then the capital.

Program 5.12
```
# read line with 2 fields
count = 0
while True:
    line = input("Enter country, capital (x to exit): ")
    if line == 'x':
        break
    else:
        list = line.split(',')
        country = list[0]
        capital = list[1]
        print ('Country: {0}\tCapital: {1}'.format(country, capital))
        count = count + 1
print ('No. of countries: ', count)
```

Sample run
```
Enter country, capital (x to exit): Malaysia, Kuala Lumpur
Country: Malaysia       Capital:  Kuala Lumpur

Enter country, capital (x to exit): Vietnam, Hanoi
Country: Vietnam        Capital:  Hanoi
Enter country, capital (x to exit): China, Beijing
Country: China  Capital:  Beijing
```

```
Enter country, capital (x to exit): Myanmar, Yangon
Country: Myanmar          Capital:  Yangon

Enter country, capital (x to exit): x
No. of countries:   4
```

Program 5.13 is similar to the above but with different data types.

Program 5.13
```
# read line with 2 input fields
line = input('Enter name, mark: ')
list = line.split(',') # split line and put fields in a list
name = list[0]
mark = int(list[1])   # convert string to integer
if mark < 50:
    grade = 'Fail'
else:
    grade = 'Pass'
print ('Name: {0}\tMark: {1}\tGrade: {2}'.format(name, mark, grade))
```

Sample run
```
Enter name, mark: Jenny, 78
Name: Jenny       Mark: 78        Grade: Pass
```

If you wish, you can ignore the numbering in the placeholders as in Program 5.14.

Program 5.14
```
# illustrates unnumbered placeholder {} and format function
name = 'Johnson'
mark = 85
grade = 'A'
print ('Name: {}\tMark: {}\tGrade: {}'.format(name, mark, grade))
```

Output
```
Name: Johnson     Mark: 85        Grade: A
```

Program 5.15 illustrates justification of output to the left, center or right using the prefix <, > and ^ respectively, given a field width of 15.

Program 5.15
```
# left, right and center justify number
n = 3456789
print('{:<15}\n{:>15}\n{:^15}'.format(n, n, n))
```

Output
```
3456789
        3456789
    3456789
```

Program 5.16 calculates and prints the area and circumference of a circle given its radius. It also illustrates formatting floating point numbers. The {:.2f} means display the output with 2 decimal places. The letter f denotes a floating point number. (Other formatting letters include d for integers and s for string.)

Also note that the format function after the control string is preceded by a period (.) The backslash (\) in the print statement tells that the statement *continues* on the next line. This is how you break a long statement into multiple lines.

Program 5.16
```
# illustrates formatting floating point numbers with {:.f}
radius = 2.75
area = 3.14 * radius**2
circumference = 2 * 3.14 * radius
print ('Radius: {:.2f}\tArea: {:.2f}\tCircumference: {:.2f}'.\
       format(radius, area, circumference))
```

Output
```
Radius: 2.75    Area: 23.75    Circumference: 17.27
```

Program 5.17 is similar but specifies the width of the output field. The {:9.2f} means print the output in 9 columns with 2 decimal places.

Program 5.17
```
n = 37.56789
print('{:9.2f}\n{:9.5f}\n{:9.0f}'.format(n, n, n))
```

Output
```
    37.57
 37.56789
       38
```

Programs 5.18 and 5.19 show how to format long numbers with a comma. The {:,} means print the number with commas (,).

Program 5.18
```
# inserting commas in numbers
n = 3456789
print('{:,}'.format(n))  #print n with comma
```

Output
```
3,456,789
```

Program 5.19
```
n = 3456789.12345
print('{:,}'.format(n))
print ('{:15.2f}'.format(n))  # print n in 15 columns with 2 dp
```

Output
```
3,456,789.12345
     3456789.12
```

Program 5.20 shows how to format numbers with zero-fills using the str() and zfill() functions. The number is first converted to string, and then prefixed with zeros to fit the width. The str(n).zfill(7) converts n to a string, and then pads the string with zeros if the lenngth is less than 7 digits long.

Program 5.20
```
# zero-fill numbers
n = 35.75
print(str(n).zfill(7))  # zero-fill if length is <= 7
n = 12345.85
print(str(n).zfill(7))  # zero-fill has no effect as length > 7
print(format(n, '012')) # another way to zero-fill
n = 123.45678
print ('Longer: {0:.5f} Shorter: {0:.2f}'.format(n))
```

Output
```
0035.75
12345.85
```

```
000012345.85
Longer: 123.45678 Shorter: 123.46
```

Program 5.21 inserts the $ sign within the control string before the placeholder for the output price.

Program 5.21
```
price = 345.75
print('Price is ${:.2f}'.format(price))
```

Output
```
Price is $345.75
```

Program 5.22 shows how to left-, right- and center-justify a string using the prefix <, > and ^ respectively, given a field width of 40.

Program 5.22
```
# print string in 40 columns - right, left and center justified
s = 'Python Programming is fun and easy'
print('{:>40}'.format(s)) # right justify
print('{:<40}'.format(s)) # left justify
print('{:^40}'.format(s)) # center justify
```

Output
```
      Python Programming is fun and easy
Python Programming is fun and easy
   Python Programming is fun and easy
```

You can combine all the three print statements into a single statement to produce the same result as follows:

```
print('{:>40}\n{:<40}\n{:^40}'.format(s, s, s))
```

Program 5.23 justifies a pattern to the right, left and center.

Program 5.23
```
# illustrates justification to right, left and center
pattern = '###$&&&'
print('{:>10}\n{:<10}\n{:^10}'.format(pattern, pattern, pattern))
```

Output
```
   ###$&&&
###$&&&
  ###$&&&
```

Program 5.24 prints rate with a percentage sign (%). It also prints floating point numbers, binary (b), octal (o) and hexadecimal (x) equivalent of values.

Program 5.24
```
rate = 0.278
print(format(rate, "%"))
print(format(123456.789, "8,.2f"))
print(format(123456.789, ",.2f"))
print(format(123456.789, ",f"))
print() # prints blank line
print(format(95, "5d")) # prints with width 5
print(format(4, "b"))    # prints binary equivalent of decimal 4
print(format(255, "x")) # prints hexadecimal equivalent of decimal 255
print(format(9, "o"))    # prints octal equivalent of decimal 9
print(format(7500, "<10d")) # left aligns number with width 10
```

Output
```
27.800000%
123,456.79
123,456.79
123,456.789000

    95
100
ff
11
7500
```

Program 5.25 shows how to format strings using placeholders with a specified width. It does that for both strings and floating point numbers. (Note: The backslash (\) in the print statement tells that the statement continues on the next line. It can be used to break a long statement into multiple lines.)

Program 5.25
```
s1 = 'No.'
s2 = 'Name'
s3 = 'Basic'
s4 = 'Rate'
s5 = 'Hours'
s6 = 'Overtime'
s7 = 'Total'
print('{:3} {:8} {:8} {:6} {:6} {:9} {:8}'.format(s1, s2, s3, s4, \
      s5, s6, s7))
v1 = 1
v2 = 'Sally'
v3 = 2500.00
v4 = 15.00
v5 = 15
v6 = v4 * v5
v7 = v3 + v6
print('{:^3} {:8} {:6.2f} {:6.2f} {:5} {:9.2f} {:9.2f}'\
      .format(v1, v2, v3, v4, v5, v6, v7))
```

Output
```
No. Name     Basic    Rate   Hours Overtime Total
  1 Sally    2500.00  15.00     15   225.00  2725.00
```

Program 5.26 illustrates escape sequences in printing dictionary items.

Program 5.26
```
tel = {'Sally': 12345, 'Lim': 23456, 'Kelly': 345667}
print ('\nTel. Directory:', tel)

print ('\nKeys:', tel.keys())

print ('\nValues:', tel.values())

print ('\nAll items in tel:', tel.items())

print ('\nAll items in tel:')
for k in tel.items():
    print(k)

print ('\nTel. keys and values:')
for k, v in tel.items():
    print(k, '\t', v)
```

```
Tel. Directory: {'Sally': 12345, 'Lim': 23456, 'Kelly': 345667}

Keys: dict_keys(['Sally', 'Lim', 'Kelly'])

Values: dict_values([12345, 23456, 345667])

All items in tel: dict_items([('Sally', 12345), ('Lim', 23456), ('Kelly',
345667)])

All items in tel:
('Sally', 12345)
('Lim', 23456)
('Kelly', 345667)

Tel. keys and values:
Sally    12345
Lim      23456
Kelly    345667
```

Program 5.27 prints dictionary items using the method keys().

Program 5.27
```
tel = {'Sally': 12345, 'Lim': 23456, 'Kelly': 345667}
print ('Lim' in tel.keys())
print ('Maria' in tel.keys())
```

Output
```
True
False
```

5.4 Reading Input from Text File

You can enter small amounts of input data using the keyboard. But for large amounts of input, it is more convenient to enter the data into a text file (using Notepad), and then make your program to read the data from the file. This will save time and effort, especially when you are testing/debugging your program. (Imagine entering the same data again and again many times until you get your code right!)

To read input data from a text file, you can use the following steps:

1) Launch Notepad and enter the data.
2) Store the file (with extension .txt) in a suitable directory (or desktop).
3) Place the cursor on the file icon, right-click, and then copy the file path.
4) Insert the file path into your program.

Program 5.25 shows how to read input data from a text file. The text file test.txt has three lines of data (shown below). Its path is

```
C:\Users\Sellappan\Desktop\test.txt
```

Copy and insert this file path in the code as follows:

```
f = open(r'C:\Users\Sellappan\Desktop\test.txt')
```

This statement will open the text file for *reading*. Note that the file path is enclosed within a pair of quotes (' '). The prefix r tells that the file path be read as *raw data*. If you don't read the path as raw data, the program will read \U as Unicode character (used to represent all the characters in all the know languages) which will produce an error message.

Once the file is opened, you can use the file object name f to reference the file within your program. It provides a short-hand notation for the file.

The f.readline() method reads the file line by line. That's why we have three readline statements to read all the data in the file.

After opening a file, it is always advisable to close it with the f.close() method.

Text file contents:

```
test.txt - Notepad
File  Edit  Format  View  Help
This is Line 1
This is Line 2
This is Line 3
```

```
# read text file line by line
# prefix r is to read raw string
f = open(r'C:\Users\Sellappan\Desktop\test.txt')
print (f.readline())
print (f.readline())
print (f.readline())
f.close()  # close the file
```

Output
```
This is Line 1

This is Line 2

This is Line 3
```

The above way of reading multiple lines of input data is very clumsy for large amounts of data. A better way is to use the for loop as in Program 5.28. The loop reads the input data line by line until the end of the file is reached (when there is no more data).

Program 5.28
```
# read input data line by line using a for loop
f = open(r'C:\Users\Sellappan\Desktop\test.txt')
for line in f:
    print (line, end = '')
f.close()
```

Output
```
This is Line 1
This is Line 2
This is Line 3
```

Better still, you can do the above using the **with open(...) as f:** statement as in Program 5.29. The with statement automatically closes the file, so it is not necessary to close the file with f.close().

Program 5.29
```
# read textfile line by line
# prefix r to read the raw string
# this is because \U starts the Unicode escape sequence
# this form of file access automatically closes the file
with open(r'C:\Users\Sellappan\Desktop\test.txt') as f:
    for line in f:
        print (line, end = '')
```

77

Output
```
This is Line 1
This is Line 2
This is Line 3
```

Program 5.30 reads input data line by line - containing the fields student name and mark - and prints the grade Pass or Fail. The first statement strips the end-of-line character (\n) which is not part of the input data. The second statement splits the line and stores the fields name and mark in rec[0] and rec[1] respectively.

```
line = line.rstrip('\n')
rec = line.split(',')
```

Text file contents:

```
mark.txt - Notepad
File   Edit   Format   View   Help
Wong,  59
John,  77
Andrew,  45
Susan,  88
Mohan,  50
Jean,  33
```

Program 5.30
```
# reads name and mark and prints the processes the results

f = open(r'C:\Users\Sellappan\Desktop\mark.txt')
print ('No. Name        Mark  Grade')
count = 0
for line in f:
    line = line.rstrip('\n')
    rec = line.split(',')
    if int(rec[1]) < 50:
        grade = "Fail"
    else:
        grade = "Pass"
    count = count + 1
    print(' {0}  {1}\t{2}  {3}'.format(count, rec[0], rec[1], grade))
f.close()
```

Output
```
No. Name        Mark  Grade
 1  Wong          59  Pass
 2  John          77  Pass
 3  Andrew        45  Fail
 4  Susan         88  Pass
 5  Mohan         50  Pass
 6  Jean          33  Fail
```

Program 5.31 is similar to the above but computes the grade using coursework, midterm and final marks.

Text file contents:

```
mark.txt - Notepad
File   Edit   Format   View   Help
Wong, 20, 15, 27
John, 30, 17, 35
Andrew, 23, 14, 40
Susan, 22, 18, 45
Mohan, 22, 15, 35
Jean, 12, 10, 15
```

Program 5.31

```python
# process exam results
print ('No. Name        Course  Midterm  Final Total  Grade')
f = open(r'C:\Users\Sellappan\Desktop\mark.txt')
count = 0
for line in f:
    line = line.rstrip('\n')
    rec = line.split(',')
    total = int(rec[1]) + int(rec[2]) + int(rec[3])
    if total < 50:
        grade = "Fail"
    else:
        grade = "Pass"
    count = count + 1
    # to continue statement on next line insert \
    print (count, ' ', rec[0], '\t', rec[1], ' ', rec[2], '  ', \
            rec[3], '  ', total, '  ', grade)
f.close()
```

Output

No.	Name	Course	Midterm	Final	Total	Grade
1	Wong	20	15	27	62	Pass
2	John	30	17	35	82	Pass
3	Andrew	23	14	40	77	Pass
4	Susan	22	18	45	85	Pass
5	Mohan	22	15	35	72	Pass
6	Jean	12	10	15	37	Fail

Program 5.32 is similar to the above but computes the grades A, B, C, etc. instead of just Pass or Fail.

Program 5.32

```python
# process exam results
f = open(r'C:\Users\Sellappan\Desktop\mark.txt')
print ('No. Name        Course  Midterm  Final Total  Grade')
count = 0
for line in f:
    line = line.rstrip('\n')
    rec = line.split(',')
    total = int(rec[1]) + int(rec[2]) + int(rec[3])
    if total < 50:
        grade = "F"
    elif total < 65:
        grade = "C"
    elif total < 85:
        grade = "B"
    else:
        grade = "A"
    count = count + 1
    print (count, ' ', rec[0], '\t', rec[1], ' ', rec[2], '  ', \
            rec[3], '  ', total, '  ', grade)
f.close()
```

Output

No.	Name	Course	Midterm	Final	Total	Grade
1	Wong	20	15	27	62	C
2	John	30	17	35	82	B
3	Andrew	23	14	40	77	B
4	Susan	22	18	45	85	A
5	Mohan	22	15	35	72	B
6	Jean	12	10	15	37	F

Program 5.33 reads employee data containing name, basic, rate and hours worked from a text file and computes their salary.

Text file contents:

```
salary.txt - Notepad
File   Edit   Format   View   Help
Wong, 1700.00, 12.00, 20
John, 1600.00, 12.00, 17
Andrew, 1500.00, 9.00, 30
Susan, 2200.00, 15.00, 15
Mohan, 2000.00, 15.00, 25
Jean, 1600.00, 11.00, 30
```

Program 5.33

```
# calculate salaries

print (' No. Name     Basic    Rate    Hours   Overtime   Total')
f = open(r'C:\Users\Sellappan\Desktop\salary.txt')

count = 0
for line in f:
    line = line.rstrip('\n')
    rec = line.split(',')
    name = rec[0]
    basic = float(rec[1])
    rate = float(rec[2])
    hours = int(rec[3])
    overtime = rate * hours
    total = basic + overtime
    count = count + 1
    print ('{:3} {:7} {:8.2f} {:6.2f} {:5} {:9.2f} {:8.2f}'.format \
        (count, name, basic, rate, hours, overtime, total))
f.close()
```

Output

No.	Name	Basic	Rate	Hours	Overtime	Total
1	Wong	1700.00	12.00	20	240.00	1940.00
2	John	1600.00	12.00	17	204.00	1804.00
3	Andrew	1500.00	9.00	30	270.00	1770.00
4	Susan	2200.00	15.00	15	225.00	2425.00
5	Mohan	2000.00	15.00	25	375.00	2375.00
6	Jean	1600.00	11.00	30	330.00	1930.00

5.5 Writing Output to Text File

To send output to a text file, open a file in the write mode 'w'. Then use the write method to send the output to the file.

The f.write method writes the contents to the file as *strings*. It accepts only one argument.
Program 5.34 illustrates this.

Program 5.34

```
# the prefix r read the raw file path string

f = open(r'C:\Users\sell780\Desktop\answer.txt', 'w')
f.write("Name: John")
f.write("\nJob: Analyst")
f.write("\nPay: $5000")
f.close()
```

Output
```
Name: John
Job: Analyst
Pay: $5000
```

Program 5.35 is similar to the above but concatenates the fields so that it becomes a single field/argument.

Program 5.35

```
f = open(r'C:\Users\sell780\Desktop\answer.txt', 'w')

# only one argument is allowed in write, so we concatenate
f.write("Product: " + "iPhone 10")
f.write("\nQuanity:" + str(57))
f.write("\nPrice: $" + str(1520.00))
f.close()
```

Output
```
Product: iPhone 10
Quanity:57
Price: $1520.0
```

Program 5.36 uses the with open (...) statement which we have already discussed earlier.

Program 5.36

```
# use with open statement that closes the file automatically after reading

with open(r'C:\Users\sell780\Desktop\answer.txt', 'w') as f:
    for i in range (1,7):
        f.write("\nThis is Line " + str(i))
```

Output
```
This is Line 1
This is Line 2
This is Line 3
This is Line 4
This is Line 5
This is Line 6
```

5.6 Reading from and Writing to Text Files

You can also read input from a text file and write output to a text file in the same program as in Program 5.37. The variable fin references the input file while the variable fout references the output file. The input for the program comes from the file mark.txt.

```
mark.txt - Notepad
File   Edit   Format   View   Help
sally,  88
chong,  55
sammy,  45
megan,  66
```

The output (shown below) is sent to the file `answer.txt`.

Program 5.37
```
# read input from text file mark.txt
# and send output to text file answer.txt
fin = open(r'C:\Users\sell780\Desktop\mark.txt')
fout = open(r'C:\Users\sell780\Desktop\answer.txt', 'w')

fout.write('\nNo. Name    Mark  Grade\n')
count = 0
for line in fin:
    line = line.rstrip('\n')
    rec = line.split(',')
    if int(rec[1]) < 50:
        grade = 'Fail'
    else:
        grade = 'Pass'
    count = count + 1
#   s = str(count) + '   ' + rec[0] + '   ' + str(rec[1]) + grade + '\n'
    fout.write('{}    {}    {}  {}\n'.format(count, rec[0], rec[1], grade))
fin.close()
fout.close()
```

Output
```
No. Name    Mark  Grade
1   sally     88  Pass
2   chong     55  Pass
3   sammy     45  Fail
4   megan     66  Pass
```

5.7 Sending Output to Printer

One way to send output to a printer is as follows:

1. Send the output to a text file.
2. Then send the text file to the printer.

This can minimize paper wastage, especially when you are testing/debugging your code.

Another way is to send the output directly to the printer. Sending output to a printer is similar to sending output to a text file. The system identifies printer(s) as LPT1, etc. To send output to a printer, use the following statement:

```
with open('LPT1:', 'w') as lpt:
    lpt.write("Hello world! ")
```

You can also do the same using the following statements:

```
lpt = open('LPT1:', 'w')
print (lpt, mytext)
close(lpt)
```

Exercise

1) Print/display the line below centre- and right-justified.

   ```
   I love Python Programming
   ```

2) Print a line with the pattern ---$$$--- repeated five times.

3) Use a single print statement to print the below information in 3 different ways as follows:

   ```
   Name: Sally, Age: 27, Email: sally@gmail.com

   Name: Sally     Age: 27       Email: sally@gmail.com

   Name: Sally
   Age: 27
   Email: sally@gmail.com
   ```

4) Send the output in (3) to a printer.

5) Print each of the integer numbers 5, 23, 95, 175 and 12345 using a field width of 7.

6) Print each of the floating point numbers 1.2345, 0.0075, 123.45 and 99.9999 using a field width of 10 and rounded to 2 decimal places.

7) Print the number 123456789 as 123,456,789.

8) Print each of these numbers 123, 45, 789, 12345 on a single line using a width of 7 with zero-fills.

9) Use numbered placeholders to print the below using a single print statement.

   Name: Johnson, Department: Accounting, Salary: 5,200.00

10) Do (8) using unnumbered placeholders.

11) Use the format function to print the numbers 1234.5678, 0.6789 and 5.12345 rounded to 2 decimal places.

12) Create a text file with 7 records (one line per record) each with the fields name, telephone and email. Write code to read and print the data.

13) Enter some data from the keyboard and send the same to a text file and to a printer.

14) Generate 200 integer random numbers in the range [1000, 9999] in an array and send the array to a text file and to a printer.

15) Convert the numbers 123, 456 and 789 to binary, octal and hexadecimal and send the output to the monitor.

Chapter 6

Built-in Functions

Learning Outcomes:

After completing this chapter, the student will be able to

- *Explain how functions work.*
- *Distinguish between built-in and user defined functions.*
- *Explain categories of functions.*
- *Call (invoke) functions.*
- *Import functions stored in modules.*

6.1 What are Functions?

A function is a small program that performs a specific task such as converting a string from lower case to uppercase, taking the square root of a number, or rounding a number to a certain number of decimal places.

A function can have zero or more parameters. Some functions may not require any parameters whereas most will require one or more parameters.

We have used the terms *function* and *method* almost interchangeably in the previous chapters, but they are not exactly the same. A method is attached to a class or class instance (classes are discussed in in chapter 8) whereas a function is not. A method uses the dot notation obj.method()while the function takes the form function_name (parameter_list).

Functions (and methods) are categorized as *built-in* (or *library*) or *programmer- or user-defined* functions (methods). Built-in functions are provided by Python; programmer-defined functions are defined by the programmers.

This chapter will discuss built-in functions (and methods), and the next chapter will discuss programmer-defined functions.

6.2 Built-in Functions

Python provide many built-in/library functions as shown in the table below.

Built-in functions

Method	Description
abs()	Returns absolute value of a number
all()	Returns True when all elements in iterable is True
any()	Returns True if any element of iterable is True
ascii()	Returns string containing printable representation
bin()	Converts integer to binary string
bool()	Coverts value to Boolean
bytearray()	Returns array of given byte size
bytes()	Returns immutable bytes object
callable()	Checks if object is callable
chr()	Returns a character (a string) from an integer

`classmethod()`	Returns class method for given function
`compile()`	Returns a Python code object
`complex()`	Creates a complex number
`delattr()`	Deletes attribute from object
`dict()`	Creates a dictionary
`dir()`	Returns attributes of object
`divmod()`	Returns a tuple of quotient and remainder
`enumerate()`	Returns an enumerate object
`eval()`	Evaluates expression
`exec()`	Executes program
`filter()`	Constructs iterator from elements which are True
`float()`	Returns floating point number from number, string
`format()`	Returns formatted representation of a value
`frozenset()`	Returns immutable frozenset object
`getattr()`	Returns value of named attribute of an object
`globals()`	Returns dictionary of current global symbol table
`hasattr()`	Returns if object has named attribute
`hash()`	Returns hash value of an object
`help()`	Calls the built-in Help system
`hex()`	Converts to integer to hexadecimal
`id()`	Returns identify of an object
`input()`	Reads and returns a line of string
`int()`	Returns integer from a number or string
`isinstance()`	Checks if an object is an instance of class
`issubclass()`	Checks if an object is subclass of a class
`iter()`	Returns iterator for an object
`len()`	Returns length of an object
`list()`	Creates a list
`locals()`	Returns dictionary of current local symbol table
`map()`	Applies function and returns a list
`max()`	Returns largest element
`memoryview()`	Returns memory view of an argument
`min()`	Returns smallest element
`next()`	Retrieves next element from iterator
`object()`	Creates a featureless object
`oct()`	Converts integer to octal
`open()`	Returns a file object
`ord()`	Returns the value of Unicode character
`pow()`	Returns x to the power of y
`print()`	Prints the given object
`property()`	Returns a property attribute
`range()`	Return sequence of integers between start and stop
`repr()`	Returns printable representation of an object
`reversed()`	Returns reversed iterator of a sequence
`round()`	Rounds a floating point number to n digits places
`set()`	Returns a set
`setattr()`	Sets value of an attribute of object
`slice()`	Creates a slice object specified by range
`sorted()`	Returns a sorted list from a given iterable
`staticmethod()`	Creates a static method from a function
`str()`	Returns string representation of an object
`sum()`	Sum items of an iterable
`super()`	Refers to base class
`tuple()`	Creates a tuple
`type()`	Returns Type of an object

`vars()`	Returns ___dict___ attribute of a class
`zip()`	Returns an iterator of tuples

The functions fall into several categories: math, string, input/output, date, lists, etc. Here, we will discuss some of these categories and some of the functions in these categories. For a more complete list, refer to Python 3.6.x documentation.)

6.3 Math Functions

Math functions (stored in the math module) are used for performing mathematical calculations such as taking the square root of a number, taking the log of a number, or rounding a number to a certain number of decimal places.

The table below gives a list of the math functions/methods.

Function/Method	Description
`abs(x)`	Returns absolute value of x.
`cos(x)`	Return the cosine of x radians.
`ceil(x)`	Return the ceiling of x, the smallest integer greater than or equal to x.
`exp(x)`	Returns the exponential value x
`factorial(x)`	Returns factorial of x
`floor(x)`	Return the floor of x, the largest integer less than or equal to x.
`log(x)`	Returns log x to base e
`log10(x)`	Returns log x to base 10
`max(s)`	Returns largest element in sequence s.
`min(s)`	Returns smallest element in sequence s.
`pow(x, y)`	Returns x raised to power of y.
`round(x, n)`	Rounds x to n decimal places.
`sqrt(x)`	Returns square root of x.
`sin(x)`	Return the sine of x radians.
`tan(x)`	Return the tan of x radians.
`trunc(x)`	Return the real value x truncated to an integer.

Programs 6.1 and 6.2 illustrate several math functions: `factorial`, `round`, `min`, `max`, etc. Note that some functions like `sqrt()` requires just one argument whereas others like `pow()` and `round()` requires two arguments.

Program 6.1
```
import math

print (abs(-3.5))                    # abs is a function
print (math.factorial (5))           # factorial is a class method
print (math.floor(9/4))
print (math.ceil(7/3))
print (math.sqrt(49))
print (math.pow(2, 5))
print (round(math.pi, 4))
print (round(math.sin(80), 4))
print (min(4, 5, 6, 7))
print (max(4, 5, 6, 7))
```

Output
```
3.5
120
2
3
```

```
7.0
32.0
3.1416
-0.9939
4
7
```

Program 6.2
```python
import math

x = [7, 3, 9, 12, 5]
print (max(x))
print (min(x))
print (sum(x))
print (sorted(x))
x.reverse()
print (x)

print (abs(-3))
print (math.sqrt(49))
print (pow(2, 3))
print (round(9/4, 2))
print (math.floor(7/5))
print (math.ceil(7/5))
print (round(math.log(12), 4))
print (round(math.log10(12), 4))
print (round(math.exp(3), 4))
print (round(math.pi, 4))
print (round(math.sin(2), 4))
```

Output
```
12
3
36
[3, 5, 7, 9, 12]
[5, 12, 9, 3, 7]
3
7.0
8
2.25
1
2
2.4849
1.0792
20.0855
3.1416
0.9093
```

6.4 String Functions

String functions are used to perform string operations, e.g., to find the length of a string, to convert a string from lower case to uppercase, to test if a string is alphanumeric, or to replace a substring in a string with another string.

The table below gives a list of string functions/methods.

Function/Method	Description
`capitalize()`	Capitalizes the first letter of string
`center(width, fillchar)`	Returns a string padded with fillchar with the original string centered to a total of width columns.
`count(str, beg = 0, end = len(string))`	Counts how many times str occurs in string or in a substring of string if starting index beg and end index end are given.
`find(str, beg = 0 end = len(string))`	Determine if str occurs in string or in a substring of string if starting index beg and end index are given; returns index if found and -1 otherwise.
`index(str, beg = 0, end = len(string))`	Same as find(), but raises an exception if str not found.
`isalpha()`	Returns True if string has at least 1 character and all characters are alphabetic and false otherwise.
`isdigit()`	Returns True if string contains only digits and False otherwise.
`islower()`	Returns True if string has at least 1 cased character and all cased characters are in lowercase and False otherwise.
`isnumeric()`	Returns True if a Unicode string contains only numeric characters and False otherwise.
`isspace()`	Returns True if string contains only whitespace characters and False otherwise.
`istitle()`	Returns True if string is properly title-cased and False otherwise.
`isupper()`	Returns True if string has at least one cased character and all cased characters are in uppercase and False otherwise.
`join(seq)`	Merges (concatenates) the string representations of elements in seq into a string, with separator string.
`len(s)`	Returns the length of string s.
`ljust(width [, fillchar])`	Returns a space-padded string with the original string left-justified to a total of width columns.
`lower(s)`	Converts all uppercase letters of s to lowercase.
`lstrip(s)`	Removes all leading whitespace in s.
`replace(old, new [, max])`	Replaces all occurrences of old in string with new or at most max occurrences if max given.
`rfind(str, beg = 0, end = len(string))`	Same as find(), but search backwards in string.
`rindex( str, beg = 0, end = len(string))`	Same as index(), but search backwards in string.
`rjust(width, [, fillchar])`	Returns a space-padded string with the original string right-justified to a total of width columns.
`rstrip(s)`	Removes all trailing whitespace of string.
`split(str='', num=string.count(str))`	Splits string according to delimiter str (space if not provided) and returns list of substrings; split into at most num substrings if given.
`splitlines('\n')`	Returns a list with all the lines in string.
`startswith(str, beg=0,end=len(string))`	Determines if string or a substring of string (if starting index beg and ending index end are given) starts with substring str; returns true if so and false otherwise.
`strip([chars])`	Performs both lstrip() and rstrip() on string
`swapcase()`	Inverts case for all letters in string.
`title(s)`	Returns title-cased version of string s: all words begin with uppercase and the rest are lowercase.
`upper(s)`	Converts lowercase letters in string s to uppercase.
`zfill (width)`	Returns original string left-padded with zeros to a total of width characters; intended for numbers, zfill() retains any sign given (less one zero).
`isdecimal(s)`	Returns True if a Unicode string s contains only decimal characters and False otherwise.

Program 6.3 illustrates several string functions/methods such as `upper`, `capitalize`, `find`, `replace`, `split`, etc.

Program 6.3

```
s = 'the universe is expanding'
s1 = 'THE uNIVERSE IS mAJESTIC'
s2 = '123'
color = 'red, yellow, green'
s3 = 'This is line 1\nThis is line 2'
s4 = '  includes blank   '

print (s.upper())
print (s.lower())
print (s.capitalize())
print (s.title())
print (s.isupper())
print (s.islower())
print (s.find('universe'))
print (s.replace('universe', 'solar system'))

print (s1.swapcase())
print (s2.isdigit())
print (s2.isnumeric())
print (s2.isalpha())

print (s.split())
print (color.split(','))
print (s3.split('\n'))

print (s4.strip())
print (s2.zfill(7))
```

Output

```
THE UNIVERSE IS EXPANDING
the universe is expanding
The universe is expanding
The Universe Is Expanding
False
True
4
the solar system is expanding
the Universe is Majestic
True
True
False
['the', 'universe', 'is', 'expanding']
['red', ' yellow', ' green']
['This is line 1', 'This is line 2']
includes blank
0000123
```

6.5 Data Conversion Functions

Data conversion functions are used to convert data from one data type to another, e.g. from string to integer or float, from integer to binary or octal, etc.

The table below gives a list of data conversion functions.

Function	Description
chr(x)	Converts an integer to a character.
complex(real [,imag])	Creates a complex number.
dict(d)	Creates a dictionary; d is a sequence of (key, value) tuples.
eval(str)	Evaluates a string and returns a value.
float(x)	Converts x to a floating-point number.
frozenset(s)	Converts s to a frozen set.
hex(x)	Converts an integer to a hexadecimal string.
int(x)	Converts x to an integer.
list(s)	Converts s to a list.
oct(x)	Converts an integer to an octal string.
ord(x)	Converts a single character to its integer value.
repr(x)	Converts x to an expression string.
set(s)	Converts s to a set.
str(x)	Converts x to a string.
tuple(s)	Converts s to a tuple.
unichr(x)	Converts an integer to a Unicode character.

Program 6.4 illustrates data conversion functions: bin, oct, hex, chr, float, list, etc.

Program 6.4
```
x = '12'
y = int(x)
z = (('aa', 5), ('bb', 7))
print (y)
print (bin(y))
print (oct(y))
print (hex(y))
print (eval('12+5'))
print (chr(77))
print (ord('5'))
print (float(y))
print (tuple(x))
print (list(x))
print (dict(z))
```

Output
```
12
0b1100
0o14
0xc
17
M
53
12.0
('1', '2')
['1', '2']
{'aa': 5, 'bb': 7}
```

6.6 Input/Output Functions

Input functions are used for reading data from the keyboard or from a text file into a program. Output functions are used to send output from a program to the monitor, file or printer.

To read data from the keyboard, use the input function. It takes the form

```
v = input ('prompt')
```

The data entered is stored in variable v.

The prompt can include escape sequences such as \n as in the following statement.

```
v = input ('\nEnter a number')
```

To send output from the program to the monitor, use the print function. It takes the form

```
print (variable list)
```

The print can include escape sequences, placeholders, and other formatting features as in Program 6.5.

Program 6.5
```
prod = 'iPhone10'
qty = 5
price = 1200.95
amount = qty * price
print (prod, qty, price, amount)
print (prod, '\t', qty, '\t', price, '\t', amount)
print ('\nProduct :', prod, '\nQuantity :', qty, '\nPrice: $', price, '\nAmount:
$', amount)
print ('\n{}\t{}\t${}\t${}'.format(prod, qty, price, amount))
print ('{}\t{}\t${:.2f}\t${:.2f}'.format(prod, qty, price, amount))
```

Output
```
iPhone10 5 1200.95 6004.75
iPhone10          5          1200.95          6004.75

Product : iPhone10
Quantity : 5
Price: $ 1200.95
Amount: $ 6004.75
iPhone10          5          $1200.95          $6004.75
iPhone10          5          $1200.95          $6004.75
```

6.7 Date Functions

Date functions allow you to manipulate dates, e.g., getting the year, month, day, hour, minute and second.

To use date functions, you need to import the datetime module as follows:

```
import datetime
```

The list of datetime class attributes and methods are as follows:

Datetime class attributes

Attribute	Description
date.min	The earliest representable date, date(MINYEAR, 1, 1).
date.max	The latest representable date, date(MAXYEAR, 12, 31).
date.resolution	The smallest possible difference between non-equal date objects, timedelta(days=1).
date.year	Between MINYEAR and MAXYEAR inclusive.
date.month	Between 1 and 12 inclusive.
date.day	Between 1 and the number of days in the given month of the given year.

Datetime class methods

Method	Description
date.today()	Returns the current local date.
date.fromtimestamp(timestamp)	Returns the local date corresponding to the POSIX timestamp.
date.fromordinal(ordinal)	Return the date corresponding to the Gregorian ordinal, where January 1 of year 1 has ordinal 1.

Programs 6.6 and 6.7 illustrate several datetime functions/methods.

Program 6.6
```
import datetime
t = datetime.time(21, 10, 30, 55)
print(t)
print('hour       :', t.hour)
print('minute     :', t.minute)
print('second     :', t.second)
print('microsecond:', t.microsecond)
print ()
today = datetime.date.today()
print(today)
print('ctime   :', today.ctime())
print('Year    :', today.year)
print('Mon     :', today.month)
print('Day     :', today.day)
print ()
tt = today.timetuple()
print('tuple   : tm_year  =', tt.tm_year)
print('          tm_mon   =', tt.tm_mon)
print('          tm_mday  =', tt.tm_mday)
print('          tm_hour  =', tt.tm_hour)
print('          tm_min   =', tt.tm_min)
print('          tm_sec   =', tt.tm_sec)
print('          tm_wday  =', tt.tm_wday)
print('          tm_yday  =', tt.tm_yday)
print('ordinal:', today.toordinal())
print('Year    :', today.year)
print('Mon     :', today.month)
print('Day     :', today.day)
```

Output
```
21:10:30.000055
hour       : 21
minute     : 10
second     : 30
microsecond: 55

2018-01-29
ctime   : Mon Jan 29 00:00:00 2018
Year    : 2018
Mon     : 1
Day     : 29
tuple   : tm_year  = 2018
          tm_mon   = 1
          tm_mday  = 29
          tm_hour  = 0
          tm_min   = 0
          tm_sec   = 0
          tm_wday  = 0
          tm_yday  = 29
ordinal: 736723
```

92

```
Year    : 2018
Mon     : 1
Day     : 29
```

Program 6.7
```
import datetime

print('Times:')
t1 = datetime.time(12, 55, 40)
print('t1: ', t1)
t2 = datetime.time(15, 5, 20)
print('t2:', t2)
print('t1 < t2?:', t1 < t2)   # date camparison
print('t1 > t2?:', t1 > t2)

print('Dates:')
d1 = datetime.date.today()
print('d1:', d1)

d2 = datetime.date.today() + datetime.timedelta(days=3)
print('d2:', d2)
print('d1 > d2?:', d1 > d2)
print('d1 < d2?:', d1 < d2)
```

Output
```
t1:   12:55:40
t2:   15:05:20
t1 < t2?: True
t1 > t2?: False
Dates:
d1: 2018-01-29
d2: 2018-02-01
d1 > d2?: False
d1 < d2?: True
```

6.8 List Functions

List functions are used to manipulate lists. For example, you can use the operators + and * for concatenating and repeating/replicating lists.

The table below gives the list functions.

List functions

Function	Description
len(list)	Gives the total length of the list.
max(list)	Returns item from the list with max value.
min(list)	Returns item from the list with min value.
list(seq)	Converts a tuple into list.

Program 6.8 illustrates list functions – len, max, min, etc.

Program 6.8
```
x = [1, 2, 3]
y = [4, 5, 6, 7]
z = ['Python']
t = ('red', 'yellow', 'green')
print (len(x))
print (max(y))
print (min(y))
```

```
print (list(t))

print (x+y)   # list concatenation
print (z*3)   # list repetition
print (5 in y) # test if 5 is in y
```

Output
```
3
7
4
['red', 'yellow', 'green']
[1, 2, 3, 4, 5, 6, 7]
['Python', 'Python', 'Python']
True
```

The table below gives list methods.

List methods

Method	Description
list.append(obj)	Appends object obj to list
list.count(obj)	Returns count of how many times obj occurs in list
list.extend(seq)	Appends the contents of seq to list
list.index(obj)	Returns the lowest index in list that obj appears
list.insert(index, obj)	Inserts object obj into list at offset index
list.pop()	Removes and returns last object or obj from list
list.remove(obj)	Removes object obj from list
list.reverse()	Reverses objects of list in place
list.sort()	Sorts objects of list, use compare func if given

Program 6.9 illustrates several list methods – append, insert, pop, sort, reverse, etc.

Program 6.9
```
x = [1, 2, 3, 3]
y = [4, 5, 6, 7]
print (x.count(3))
x.append(55)
print (x)
x.extend(y)
print (x)
print (y.index(6))
y.insert(3, 99)
print (y)
y.pop()
print (y)
y.remove(6)
print (y)
y.reverse()
print (y)
y.sort()
print (y)
```

Output
```
2
[1, 2, 3, 3, 55]
[1, 2, 3, 3, 55, 4, 5, 6, 7]
2
[4, 5, 6, 99, 7]
[4, 5, 6, 99]
[4, 5, 99]
[99, 5, 4]
[4, 5, 99]
```

6.9 Tuple Functions

Like lists, you can use the + and * operators for concatenating and repeating tuples.

Tuple functions operate on tuples and are similar to list functions.

Tuple functions

Function	Description
len(tuple	Gives the length of the tuple.
max(tuple)	Returns item from the tuple with max value.
min(tuple)	Returns item from the tuple with min value.
tuple(seq)	Converts a list into a tuple.

Program 6.10 illustrates several tuple functions.

Program 6.10

```
x = (1, 2, 3)
y = (4, 5, 6, 7)
z = ['Python']
t = ['red', 'yellow', 'green']
print (len(x))
print (max(y))
print (min(y))
print (tuple(t))

print (x+y)  # list concatenation
print (z*3)  # list repetition
print (3 in x) # check if 3 is in x
```

Output

```
3
7
4
('red', 'yellow', 'green')
(1, 2, 3, 4, 5, 6, 7)
['Python', 'Python', 'Python']
True
```

6.10 Dictionary Functions

Dictionary functions and methods are used to manipulate dictionaries. The tables below give a list of dictionary functions and methods.

Dictionary functions

Function	Description
len(dict)	Gives the length of the dictionary.
str(dict)	Returns a printable string representing dictionary.
type(dict)	Returns the type of the passed variable.

Dictionary methods

Method	Description
d.clear()	Removes all elements of dictionary
d.copy()	Returns a shallow copy of dictionary
d.fromkeys()	Create a new dictionary with keys from seq and values .

d.get(key, default=None)	For key, returns value or default if key not in dictionary
d.items()	Returns a list of d (key, value) pairs
d.keys()	Returns list of dictionary keys
d.setdefault(key, default = None)	Similar to get(), but will set d[key] = default if key is not already in d
d.update(dict2)	Adds dictionary key-values pairs
d.values()	Returns list of dictionary values

Program 6.11 illustrates several dictionary functions and methods.

Program 6.11
```
teldir = {'john': '111', 'sam': '222', 'May': '333'}
print (teldir)
print (teldir.items())
print (teldir.keys())
print (teldir.values())
new = {'jun': '444'}
teldir.update(new)
print (teldir.items())
teldir.clear()
print (teldir)
```

Output
```
{'john': '111', 'sam': '222', 'May': '333'}
dict_items([('john', '111'), ('sam', '222'), ('May', '333')])
dict_keys(['john', 'sam', 'May'])
dict_values(['111', '222', '333'])
dict_items([('john', '111'), ('sam', '222'), ('May', '333'), ('jun', '444')])
{}
```

6.11 Set Functions

Set functions and methods manipulate sets. The tables below give a list of these functions and methods.

Function/Method	Equivalent to	Description
len(s)		Returns number of elements in set s
x in s		Test x for membership in s
x not in s		Test x for non-membership in s
s.issubset(t)	s <= t	Test if every element in s is in t
s.issuperset(t)	s >= t	Test if every element in t is in s
s.union(t)	s | t	New set with elements from both s and t
s.intersection(t)	s & t	New set with elements common to s and t
s.difference(t)	s - t	New set with elements in s but not in t
s.symmetric_difference(t)	s ^ t	New set with elements in either s or t but not both
s.copy()		New set with a shallow copy of s
s.update(t)	s |= t	Return set s with elements added from t
s.intersection_update(t)	s &= t	Return set s keeping only elements also found in t
s.difference_update(t)	s -= t	Return set s after removing elements found in t
s.symmetric_difference_update(t)	s ^= t	Return set s with elements from s or t but not both
s.add(x)		Add element x to set s
s.remove(x)		Remove x from set s
s.discard(x)		Removes x from set s if present
s.pop()		Remove and return an arbitrary element from s
s.clear()		Remove all elements from set s

Program 6.12 illustrates several functions and methods.

Program 6.12
```
v = set(['a', 'e', 'i', 'o', 'u'])
v2 = set (['a', 'e'])
e = set([2, 4, 6, 8, 'e', 'u'])
print (len(v))
print ('x' in v)
print ('y' not in v)
print (v | e)    # union
print (v-e)      # difference
print (v & e)    # intersection
print (v2 <= v)
print (v < v2)

s = set([99])
v.update(s)
print (v)
v.remove(99)
print (v)
v.add(77)
print (v)
```

Output
```
5
False
True
{'e', 2, 4, 6, 8, 'u', 'o', 'a', 'i'}
{'o', 'a', 'i'}
{'e', 'u'}
True
False
{'e', 99, 'u', 'o', 'a', 'i'}
{'e', 'u', 'o', 'a', 'i'}
{'e', 'u', 77, 'o', 'a', 'i'}
```

6.12 Sample Programs

This section gives several sample programs to help you grasp the material presented in this chapter.

Program 6.13 performs several things: calculates the average and maximum mark of students, prints their names and marks in alphabetical order of names. The `sorted` function sorts the results.

Program 6.13
```
name = ['Joe', 'Wong', 'Sally', 'Zoe', 'Sam']
mark = [59, 82, 77, 45, 95]
print ('name:', name)
print ('mark:', mark)
n = len(name)                # get list length
print ('average =', round(sum(mark)/n, 2)) # 2 functions applied
print ('maximum =', max(mark)) # 1 function

pair = zip(name, mark) # pair name and mark lists
score = tuple(pair)  # convert to tuple
print (score)

print ('\nunsorted')
for s, m in score:
    print(s, m)
```

```
print ('\nsorted')
for s, m in sorted(score):   # sorted on name
    print(s, m)
```

Output
```
name: ['Joe', 'Wong', 'Sally', 'Zoe', 'Sam']
mark: [59, 82, 77, 45, 95]
average = 71.6
maximum mark = 95
(('Joe', 59), ('Wong', 82), ('Sally', 77), ('Zoe', 45), ('Sam', 95))
unsorted
Joe 59
Wong 82
Sally 77
Zoe 45
Sam 95

sorted
Joe 59
Sally 77
Sam 95
Wong 82
Zoe 45
```

▪ **all iterable**

The all() function returns True if all the elements evaluates to True and False otherwise.

Program 6.14 illustrates this.

Program 6.14
```
mylist = [1, 2, 3, 4, 5, 6]
print (all(mylist))

mylist.append(0)       # 0 evaluates to False
print (all(mylist))

mylist.append('')      # null/space evaluates to False
print (all(mylist))

l2 = []                # empty list evaluates to True
print (all(l2))

t1 = ('joyful')        # all letters evaluate to True
print (all(t1))

t2 = ('joyful', '')    # null/space evaluates to False
print (all(t2))

s = {}                 # empty list evaluates to True
print (all(s))
```

Output
```
True
False
False
True
True
False
True
```

98

- **any(iterable)**

The any() function returns True if any element of the iterable evaluates to True; otherwise it returns False.

Program 6.15 illustrates this.

Program 6.15
```
mylist = [1, 2, 3, 4, 5, 6]
print (any(mylist))

mylist.append(0)
print (any(mylist))

mylist.append('')
print (any(mylist))

l2 = []                    # empty list evaluates to False
print (any(l2))
t1 = ('joyful')
print (any(t1))
t2 = ('joyful', '')
print (any(t2))
t3 = ()                    # empty list evaluates to False
print (any(t3))
s = {}                     # empty list evaluates to False
print (any(s))
```

Output
```
True
True
True
False
True
True
False
False
```

- **zip(*iterables)**

The zip() function takes the iterable and combines respective elements from each of the iterables into a new iterable object.

Programs 6.16 and 6.17 illustrate this.

Program 6.16
```
prod = ['aaa', 'bbb', 'ccc', 'ddd', 'eee']
price = [1.1, 2.2, 3.3, 4.4, 5.5]
print (prod)
print (price)
pair = list(zip(prod, price))
print (pair)
```

Output
```
['aaa', 'bbb', 'ccc', 'ddd', 'eee']
[1.1, 2.2, 3.3, 4.4, 5.5]
[('aaa', 1.1), ('bbb', 2.2), ('ccc', 3.3), ('ddd', 4.4), ('eee', 5.5)]
```

Program 6.17
```
color = ('red', 'yellow', 'green')
code = ('r', 'y', 'g')
```

```
print (color)
print (code)
pair = list(zip(color, code))
print (pair)
```

Output
```
('red', 'yellow', 'green')
('r', 'y', 'g')
[('red', 'r'), ('yellow', 'y'), ('green', 'g')]
```

- **sorted(iterable)**

The sorted(iterable) returns a new sorted list from the items in iterable. This arranges lists, tuples, and sets in a known order.

Program 6.18 illustrates this.

Program 6.18
```
name = ['zoe', 'sally', 'john', 'zul', 'wong']
pair = {'joe': 111, 'wong': 222, 'zul': 333}
color = ('yellow', 'purple', 'green', 'red')
num = [55, 77, 22, 99, 222, 11]
print (sorted(name))
print (sorted(pair))
print (sorted(color))
print (sorted(num))
```

Output
```
['john', 'sally', 'wong', 'zoe', 'zul']
['joe', 'wong', 'zul']
['green', 'purple', 'red', 'yellow']
[11, 22, 55, 77, 99, 222]
```

- **chr(i)**

The chr() function returns the ASCII code of an integer i (i must be in the range 0 to 255). This function is the inverse of the ord() function.

Program 6.19 illustrates this function.

Program 6.19
```
print (chr(65))
print (ord('A'))
print (ord(chr(65)))
print (chr(ord('A')))
```

Output
```
A
65
65
A
```

- **ord(s)**

The ord() function is the inverse of the chr() function. Given a string of length one, it returns an integer representing the ordinal value of that character. If the string length is greater than one, it does that for each character.

Program 6.20 illustrates this.

Program 6.20
```
alpha = 'ABCDEF'
alpha = 'abcdef'
for letter in alpha:
    print(ord(letter), letter)
```

Output
```
97  a
98  b
99  c
100 d
101 e
102 f
```

- **@classmethod**

The @classmethod is a decorator for a class method to make the first parameter to receive a reference to the class itself (as opposed to instance). The distinction between @classmethod and @staticmethod is that if a static method wishes to reference a class variable, it must know the class name.

Program 6.21 illustrates this.

Program 6.21
```
class MyClass(object):
    x = 20
    @classmethod
    def f1(cls):    # reference to class, not to instance
        return 2 * cls.x  #

    @staticmethod
    def f2():
        return 2 * MyClass.x  # access class variable

print (MyClass.f1())
print (MyClass.f2())

class MySubClass(MyClass):
    x = 15

# main
print (MySubClass.f1())
print (MySubClass.f2())
```

Output
```
40
40
30
40
```

Exercise

1. Given x = 3, y = 5, z = 123.45, write code to perform the following:

   (a) Square of x
   (b) x raised to the power of y
   (c) Square root of z
   (d) Log10 of z
   (e) e^x

2. Given s1 = 'It is a beautiful day!', s2 = 'summer and winter, spring time and autumn', write code to perform the following:

   (a) Convert s1 to uppercase
   (b) Find the length of s2
   (c) Concatenate s1 and s2
   (d) How many 'a's are in s2?
   (e) Replace 'beautiful' with 'gorgeous' in s1
   (f) Remove all spaces from string s1.

3. Generate 200 integer random numbers in the range [1000, 9999]:

   (a) How many of these numbers are between (a) 1000 and 4999 and (b) 5000 and 9999?
   (b) How many of these are even numbers?
   (c) How many of these numbers are divisible by 7?

4. Given x = [23, 67, 99, 205, 49, 125], y = [-3, 45, -29, 99], write code to perform the following:

   (a) Find the maximum value in x
   (b) Compute the sum of elements in x
   (c) Multiply each item in y by 7
   (d) Append y to x
   (e) Sort x in ascending order.

5. Given t1 = ('malaysia', 'vietnam', 'myanmar', 'cambodia', 'india'), t2 = ('my', 'vn', 'mm', 'kh', in'), write code to perform the following:

   (a) Print the corresponding items in t1 and t2
   (b) Print items from t1[2] to the end
   (c) Print t1 in reverse order.

6. Given d = {'iPhone': 1200, 'laptop': 2500, 'desktop': 2900}, perform the following tasks:

   (f) Print all the items in d
   (g) Print all the keys in d
   (h) Print the key 'desktop' and its value
   (i) Add the pairs 'GPU': 15000 and 'Mainframe': 50000
   (j) Remove 'Mainframe' and its value.

7. Given set s = ['a', 'e', 'i', 'o', 'u'], perform the following tasks:

   (a) Is 'x' in s?
   (b) Is 'U' in s?
   (c) Is 'e' in s?

8. Give two matrices, perform the following tasks:

$$x = \begin{array}{ccc} 2 & -3 & 5 \\ 1 & 9 & 4 \\ 3 & -1 & 7 \end{array} \qquad y = \begin{array}{ccc} -5 & 1 & 0 \\ 3 & 6 & 2 \\ 1 & 3 & 8 \end{array}$$

(a) Multiply x and y and store the result in z
(b) Transpose x and store it in v
(c) Take the inverse of x and store in w
(d) Find the determinant of x.

9. Solve the following linear equations:

$x - 3y + 2z = 4$
$2x + 4y - z = 3$
$3x - y + 5z = -5$

10. Given four students and their marks in three courses (as follows), perform the following tasks:

x = ['joe', [55, 77, 99], 'sam', [45, 66, 88], 'sally', [60, 80, 90], 'may', [45, 70, 85]]

(a) Print in one line each student's name and marks
(b) Calculate each student's name, total and average mark.

11. Given a collection n=10 books with their reference number and titles. Write a program using dictionary to perform the following tasks:

(a) List the entire collection
(b) Given a reference number, display its title
(c) Append two books with their reference
(d) Delete a book given its reference.

12. Print the current date and obtain the following: Year, Month, Day, Hours, Minutes, Seconds.

Chapter 7

User-defined Functions

Learning Outcomes:

After completing this chapter, the student will be able to

- *Define functions.*
- *Call functions as statement and as expression*
- *Call functions by value and by reference*
- *Return values from functions.*
- *Overload functions.*
- *Define recursive functions.*
- *Define anonymous functions.*

7.1 Why User-defined Functions?

Python provides lots of standard functions that programmers/users need to develop their software applications. However, it doesn't provide all the functions that they will ever need. So Python lets users to define their own functions and call them as and when they need.

Functions are coded (written) once but used many times. They are reusable code. You can call them any number of times anywhere in your program. You can even store them in a file and call them later in other programs.

Using functions has two main benefits:

- It supports modularity - software developers can break a complex application into smaller chunks (functions), write code for them, and combine them so they work as a single system.

- It simplifies software maintenance - as functions are compact, they are easier to code, test/debug and document.

7.2 Defining Functions

A function in Python is defined using the keyword `def`. It takes the form

```
def function-name(parameter list):
    statement(s) # function body/block
    [return expression]
```

The parameter list consists of zero or more parameters. The function body is a block of statements, indented by a fixed number of blanks (typically four). The function body is executed when the function is called.

Parameters in a function can be mandatory or optional. Optional parameters (if any) must always follow the mandatory parameters. In other words, mandatory parameters precede the optional parameters in the parameter list.

104

The function body can have one or more return statements and they can appear anywhere in the body. The return statement if present terminates the function call and returns the result to the calling function. If the return statement has no value, the value None is returned. If the function has no return statement, the function terminates when it reaches the end and the value None is returned.

The following are some rules for defining functions:

- Functions begin with the keyword def followed by the function-name and parentheses ().

- The function parameters must be placed inside the parentheses (). You can also define parameters inside the parentheses.

- The function block starts with a colon (:) and is indented by fixed number of spaces (typically 4 spaces).

- The return statement terminates the function and returns a value (if any) to the calling function. A return statement without an expression returns None.

7.3 Calling Functions

When a function *calls* (or invokes) another function, the computer temporarily suspends the execution of the current function and branches off to execute the *called* function. After the called function completes/terminates, control reverts back to the *calling* function as shown in the diagram below.

Control flow between calling function and called function
Calling function as expression, statement, or expression inside a print statement

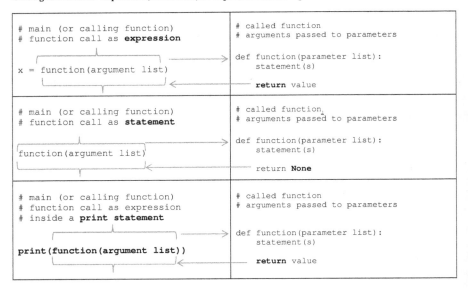

Functions can be called in three ways as shown in the above figure:

1) As an *expression* on the right hand side of the assignment operator = in an assignment statement

2) As a single statement

3) As an expression inside a print statement

The rows in the figure show the three ways of calling a function.

Program 7.1 calls the find_length function as an *expression* on the right hand side of the assignment operator (=). It passes one argument/parameter (s) of type string. The function returns the length of the string.

Program 7.1
```
# calling function as an expression
# function
def find_length(s):
    return (len(s))   # returns result

# main function
while (True):
    s = input('Enter a string: ')
    n = find_length(s) # function call as expression
    if n > 0:
        print ("Length of string '{0}' = {1}".format(s, n))
    else:
        break
print ('Finished')
```

Sample Output
```
Enter a string: gorgeous day
Length of string 'gorgeous day' = 12

Enter a string: beautiful day
Length of string 'beautiful day' = 13

Enter a string: rainy day
Length of string 'rainy day' = 9

Enter a string:
Finished
```

Program 7.2 calls the print_heading function as a *statement* (not as an expression as in the previous example). It passes no arguments/parameters, so function returns None.

Program 7.2
```
# calling function as a statement
# function
def print_heading(): # no parameter
    print ('Global Solutions Provider Sdn. Bhd.')
    # [returns None]

# main function
print ('Page 1')
print_heading()
print () # print empty line
print ('Page 2')
print_heading()
```

Output
```
Page 1
Global Solutions Provider Sdn. Bhd.

Page 2
Global Solutions Provider Sdn. Bhd.
```

Program 7.3 calls the `triangle_area` function inside the `format` function which is inside the print function. This is an example of nested functions. The output is formatted to 4 decimal places.

Program 7.3
```
# calling function inside a print statement
# function
def triangle_area(base, height):
    area = 0.5 * base * height
    return area

# main function
base = 4.5
height = 6.8
print ('Area of triangle: {:.4f}'.format (triangle_area(base, height)))
```

Output
```
Area of triangle: 15.3000
```

7.4 Call by Value vs. Reference

Python passes all arguments as *pointers to objects*. In some cases, these pointers are *passed as values* while in other cases they are *passed as references*.

When a pointer variable/argument is *passed as value*, the function creates a *local copy* (parameter) which exists only during the *lifetime* or scope of the function. Any change made to the parameter does *not* affect the argument in the calling function as they are two *different* variables.

When a pointer variable/argument is *passed as reference*, the function does *not* create a local copy. It uses the argument as the parameter. Any change to the parameter automatically *changes* the argument value in the calling function as they both are one and the *same* variable.

The diagrams below illustrate calling by value and calling by reference.

Call by value

Calling function

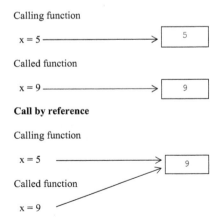

Call by reference

107

But we really haven't answered the question: when is a function called by value, and when is it called by reference?

The general rule is: pointer references to *immutable* objects like numbers and strings are *called by value* and pointer references to *mutable* objects like lists are *called by reference*.

Here are some examples to illustrate these two types of function calls.

Program 7.4 illustrates *calling function by value*. The changeval() function *changes* the value of x (an immutable object) from 5 to 7. The scope of x is *local* to the function. Outside the function, x retains its original value (5).

Program 7.4
```
# passing pointer as value, calling function by value

# function
def changeval(x):
    x = 7   # x is changed, so its scope is local
    print ('Value inside function is', x)
    return x

# main
x = 5
print ('Value of x before function call:', x)
# name is passed as value
print ('Value of x after function call:', changeval (x))
print ('Original value of x:', x) # original value is unchanged
```

Output
```
Value of x before function call: 5
Value inside function is 7
Value of x after function call: 7
Original value of x: 5
```

Program 7.5 produces the same output even though it uses different names for argument (y) and parameter (x). It doesn't really matter if the names are same or different. However, to avoid confusion, it is advisable to use the same name.

Program 7.5
```
# using different names for argument and parameter

# function
def changeval(x):
    x = 7   # x is changed, so its scope is local
    print ('Value of x inside function:', x)
    return x

# main function
y = 5
print ('Value of y before function call:', y)
# name is passed as value
print ('Value of y after function call:', changeval (y))
print ('Original value of y:', y) # original value is unchanged
```

Output
```
Value of y before function call: 5
Value inside function is 7
Value of y after function call: 7
Original value of y: 5
```

Program 7.6 is similar to the above. Here, a string (another immutable object) is passed, instead of a number.

Program 7.6
```
# passing pointer to a string object, calling function by value

# function
def changeid(name):
    name = "John"   # name is changed, so its scope is local
    print ('Name inside function:', name)
    return name

# main function
name = "Johnson"
print ('Name before function call:', name)
# name is passed as value
print ('Name after function call:', changeid (name))
# the original name is not changed
print ('Original name:', name) # original name is unchanged
```

Output
```
Name before function call: Johnson
Name inside function: John
Name after function: John
Original name: Johnson
```

Program 7.7 illustrates *calling function by reference*. The object pointer to `mylist` (a mutable object) is passed by reference. Any change made to the parameter also affects the argument. That means `mylist` has a global scope.

Program 7.7
```
# passing pointer to a list (a mutable object), calling by reference
# calling function by reference

# function
def newlist(mylist):
    mylist.append ([5, 6, 7])
    print ('mylist inside function:', mylist)
    return mylist

# main
mylist = [1, 2, 3, 4]
print ('mylist before function call:', mylist)
print ('mylist after function call:', newlist(mylist))
print ('new mylist!', mylist) # mylist is changed!
```

Output
```
mylist before function call: [1, 2, 3, 4]
mylist inside function: [1, 2, 3, 4, [5, 6, 7]]
mylist after function call: [1, 2, 3, 4, [5, 6, 7]]
new mylist! [1, 2, 3, 4, [5, 6, 7]]
```

Program 7.8 is similar to the above.

Program 7.8
```
# passing pointer to a list (a mutable object), calling by reference

# function
def changelist(x):
    x[2] = 20
    print ('Value of x inside function:', x)
    return x
```

```
# main
x = [1, 2, 3, 4, 5]
print ('Value of x before function call:', x)
print ('Value of x after function call:', changelist (x))
print ('Value of altered list after function call:', x)
```

Output
```
Value of x before function call: [1, 2, 3, 4, 5]
Value of x inside function: [1, 2, 20, 4, 5]
Value of x after function call: [1, 2, 20, 4, 5]
Value of altered list after function call: [1, 2, 20, 4, 5]
```

Program 7.9 illustrates multiple function definitions. All the function calls take the form of statements.

Program 7.9
```
# illustrates multiple functions

def function1(s):
    print ('String:', s)

def function2(s, n):
    print ('String:{}\tNumber:{}'.format (s, n))

def function3(s, n, b):
    print ('String: {}\tNumber: {}\tBoolean: {}'.format(s, n, b))

s = 'heart-wrenching story'
n = 777
b = True
function1(s)
function2(s, n)
function3(s, n, b)
```

Output
```
String: heart-wrenching story
String:heart-wrenching story       Number:777
String: heart-wrenching story      Number: 777       Boolean: True
```

7.4 Function Overloading

A function is said to be *overloaded* if it has the *same name* but has different number of parameters and/or types.

Overloading functions in Python is slightly different from other languages. The special parameter *args (a tuple) specifies the parameter list, which can be zero or more (the prefix * means zero or more).

Program 7.10 illustrates function overloading. The variable count counts the number of parameters in *args. The if...elif...else statement then calls the appropriate print () method based on the number/type of parameters.

Program 7.10
```
# illustrates function overloading

# *args is a string with zero or more parameters
def print_all(*args):
    count = len(args)
    if count == 1:
        print (args[0:1])
```

```
    elif count == 2:
         print (args[0:2])
    elif count == 3:
         print (args[0:3])
    else:
         print (args[0:4])
print_all('joe')
print_all('joe', 25)
print_all('joe', 25, 70.5)
print_all('joe', 25, 70.5, True)
```

Output
```
()
('joe',)
('joe', 25)
('joe', 25, 70.5)
('joe', 25, 70.5, True)
```

7.5 Scope of Variables

Variables in Python can have a global or local scope. By default all variables are local, unless they are declared *explicitly* as global.

Variables inside a function are local to that function. Updating them inside the function will have no effect on other variables outside the function even if they have the same name.

Unlike in other programming languages, variables in Python are declared *implicitly* when they are assigned values. For example, if you assign an integer to x, then x will be of type int, and so on.

Here are some examples.

Program 7.11
```
x = 5          # x is declared implicitly as type int
y = 7.92       # y is of type float
z = True       # z is of type bool
s = 'nice'     # s is of type str
```

Global vs. Local in Functions

You can make a variable global from inside a function by assigning a value to it outside the function as in Program 7.12

Program 7.12
```
def f():
    print(s)   # s has a global scope
# main()
s = 'I love Malaysia!'
f()
```

Output
```
I love Malaysia!
None
```

Or you can make a variable local by declaring it implicitly in the function as in Program 7.13.

Program 7.13
```
def f(s):
    print(s)        # s has local a scope

s = 'I love Malaysia!'
f(s)
```

This produces the same output.

Program 7.14
```
def f(s):
    s = 'I love Malaysia!'  # s has local scope
    print(s)

s = 'I love Vietnam!'
f(s)
print (s)
```

Output
```
I love Malaysia!
I love Vietnam!
```

Program 7.15 declares variable s as global inside the function using the keyword global. From that point onwards, s takes on a global scope, storing the latest value whether assigned inside or outside the function.

Program 7.15
```
def f():
    global s
    print(s)
    s = 'I love Malaysia'
    print(s)

s = 'I love Vietnam!'
f()
print(s)

s = 'I love Yangon'
f()
print (s)
```

Output
```
I love Vietnam!
I love Malaysia
I love Malaysia
I love Yangon
I love Malaysia
I love Malaysia
```

7.6 Recursive Functions

A **recursive** function is one that *calls itself* repeatedly until an ***anchor condition*** terminates it.

Here are three examples of recursive functions.

- **Factorial of a number**

The *factorial* of a natural number, which is given by

```
factorial(n) = 1                      for n = 0
             = n * factorial(n-1)     for n > 0
```

If n=0, the value of factorial(n) = 1. This is the *anchor* condition for the function. In recursion, you must always have an anchor, otherwise the function will not terminate. If n>0, the function calls itself recursively with a new value of n.

Program 7.16 illustrates defining and calling recursive functions.

Program 7.16
```
# function to compute factorial recursively

def factorial(n):
    if n < 1:
        return 1
    else:
        return n * factorial(n - 1)   # calls function recursively

while True:
    n = int(input("Enter a small integer (0 to exit): "))
    fact = factorial(n)   # call the function
    print ("The factorial of {0} = {1}".format(n, fact))
```

Sample Output
```
Enter a small integer (0 to exit): 7
The factorial of 7 = 5040

Enter a small integer (0 to exit): 13
The factorial of 13 = 6227020800

Enter a small integer (0 to exit): 19
The factorial of 19 = 121645100408832000

Enter a small integer (0 to exit): 0
The factorial of 0 = 1

Enter a small integer (0 to exit):
```

- **Fibonacci sequence**

Another example of recursion is the Fibonacci sequence: 1, 1, 2, 3, 5, 8, 13, 21.... Here each number after the first two is the *sum* of the two *preceding* numbers.

Program 7.17 illustrate this.

Program 7.17
```
# function to generate Fibonacci sequence recursively

def fib(n):
    if n <= 1:
        return n
    else:
        return (fib(n-1) + fib(n-2)) # fib() calls itself recursively

# main function
```

```
print ("Fibonacci sequence: ")
while (True):
    n = int(input("\nEnter an integer number (0 to exit): "))
    if n == 0:
        break
    else:
        for i in range (n):
            print (fib(i), end = ' ')   # calls fib() function
print ("\nFinished")
```

Sample Output
```
Fibonacci sequence:

Enter an integer number (0 to exit): 8
0 1 1 2 3 5 8 13

Enter an integer number (0 to exit): 17
0 1 1 2 3 5 8 13 21 34 55 89 144 233 377 610 987

Enter an integer number (0 to exit): 0

Finished
```

▪ **Hanoi Tower Game**

While you can many programs without using recursion, some programs are best written using recursion, e.g., the Hanoi Tower game problem (illustrated in the below diagram). This problem is best solved by using recursion.

Hanoi Tower Game

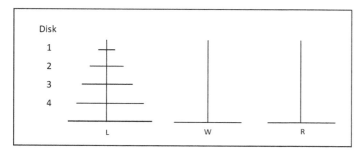

This game uses three pegs L, W and R (for Left/Source, Work and Right/Destination) and a set of disks of varying sizes. Initially, all disks are in peg L, and they are arranged from the largest at the bottom to the smallest at the top (as in the figure below). The task is to transfer the disks, one by one, from peg L to peg R using work peg W given the rule that the disks at each peg must always be arranged from the largest at the bottom to the smallest at the top.

The algorithm to solve this problem is as follows:

1. If n=1, move the single disk from L to R and stop.
2. Move the top n-1 disks from L to W, using R as work peg.
3. Move the remaining disks from L to R.
4. Move the n-1 disks from W to R, using L as work peg.

Program 7.18 shows the code for solving this problem. The three disks are s (source), d (destination) and w (work). The s and d correspond to L and R in the diagram.

Program 7.18

```
# function to solve Hanoi Tower problem recursively

# s = source (left peg), d = destination (right peg), w = work (peg)

def transfer (n, s, d, w):
    if n == 1:
        print ("Move disk 1 from peg {0} to peg {1}".format(s, d))
    else:
        # move n-1 disks from source to work
        transfer(n - 1, s, w, d) # call transfer recursively
        print ("Move disk {0} from peg {1} to peg {2}".format(n,s,d))
        # move n-1 disks from work to destination
        transfer(n - 1, w, d, s)

# main function
n = int(input("Enter number of disks: "))
if n > 0:
    s, d, w = 'L', 'R', 'W' # L = left peg, R = Right peg, W = Work peg
    transfer(n, s, d, w)
```

Sample Output

```
Enter number of disks: 4
Move disk 1 from peg L to peg W
Move disk 2 from peg L to peg R
Move disk 1 from peg W to peg R
Move disk 3 from peg L to peg W
Move disk 1 from peg R to peg L
Move disk 2 from peg R to peg W
Move disk 1 from peg L to peg W
Move disk 4 from peg L to peg R
Move disk 1 from peg W to peg R
Move disk 2 from peg W to peg L
Move disk 1 from peg R to peg L
Move disk 3 from peg W to peg R
Move disk 1 from peg L to peg W
Move disk 2 from peg L to peg R
Move disk 1 from peg W to peg R
```

7.7 Anonymous Functions

Anonymous functions are small functions defined on a single line. These functions don't use the keyword def. Instead, they use the keyword lambda. Lambda expressions can take many arguments, but returns only one value.

Lambda functions take the form

```
lambda [arg1 [,arg2,.....argn]]: expression
```

Here is an example with its output.

Example

```
avg = lambda x1, x2, x3: (x1 + x2 + x3)/3
print (round(avg(15, 22, 37), 2))
```

Output
```
24.67
```

7.8 Sample Programs

This section gives you more examples of user-defined functions.

Program 7.19 uses the `spc(n)` function to generate n spaces. This function is useful in printing output.

Program 7.19
```
# space function to generate n spaces

def spc(n):
    s = ''
    for i in range (n):
        s = s + ' '
    return s

c1 = 'No.'
c2 = 'Name'
c3 = 'Mark'
c4 = 'Grade'
print (c1, spc(3), c2, spc(10), c3, spc(3), c4)
```

Output
```
No.    Name         Mark    Grade
```

Program 7.20 illustrates a palindrome. A *palindrome* is a string (e.g., a sentence, phrase or number) where reading it backward and reading forward is the same. For example, the strings madam and sagas and the numbers 12344321, 1234321 are palindromes whereas gorgeous and 12345 are not.

Program 7.20
```
# uses multiple functions

# palindrome function
def palindrome(s):
    rs = ''.join(reversed(s))  # reverses string
    if rs == s:
        return (True)
    else:
        return (False)

# length function
def find_length(s):
    return (len(s))  # returns result

# main function
while (True):
    s = input('Enter a string: ')
    n = find_length(s) # calls length function
    if n > 0:
        if palindrome(s):  # calls palindrome function
            yn = 'Yes'
        else:
            yn = 'No'
        print ("Is {0} a palindrome? {1}".format(s, yn))
    else:
        break
print ('Finished')
```

```
Enter a string: 123454321
Is 123454321 a palindrome? Yes

Enter a string: abccde
Is abccde a palindrome? No

Enter a string: abcba
Is abcba a palindrome? Yes

Enter a string: Madam
Is Madam a palindrome? No

Enter a string: madam
Is madam a palindrome? Yes

Enter a string: sagas
Is sagas a palindrome? Yes

Enter a string:
Finished
```

Program 7.21 calculates the area and circumference of a circle given the radius.

Program 7.21
```
# illustrates multiple functions
# function definitions
# calculate area
def area(r):
    return 3.14*r*r

# calculate circumference
def circum(r):
    return 2.0*3.14*r

# main function
while (True):
    radius = float(input("Enter radius: "))
    if (radius > 0):
        print ('Area = {:.2f}'.format(area(radius)))
        print ('Circumference = {:.2f}'.format(circum(radius)))
    else:
        break
print ("Finished")
```

Sample Output
```
Enter radius: 5.5
Area = 94.98
Circumference = 34.54

Enter radius: 2.8
Area = 24.62
Circumference = 17.58
Enter radius: 0
Finished
```

Program 7.22 calculates the area and circumference of a circle using a single function. The function returns two results – area and circumference – using a single `return` statement.

Program 7.22
```
# this function returns multiple values
def circle(r):
```

117

```
    area = 3.14 * r * r
    circum = 2 * 3.14 * r
    return (area, circum) # returns multiple values

while (True):
    radius = float(input("Enter radius (0 to exit): "))
    if radius <= 0:
        break
    else:
        a, c = circle(radius)   # assigns to 2 variables
        print ("Area = {:.2f}".format(a))
        print ("Circumference = {:.2f}".format(c))
print ("Done")
```

Sample Output
```
Enter radius (0 to exit): 5.5
Area = 94.98
Circumference = 34.54

Enter radius (0 to exit): 7.8
Area = 191.04
Circumference = 48.98

Enter radius (0 to exit): 12.45
Area = 486.71
Circumference = 78.19

Enter radius (0 to exit): 0
Done
```

Program 7.23 prints a specified number of blank lines (useful for printing reports).

Program 7.23
```
# prints specified no. of blank lines

# function
def newline(n):
    for i in range (n):
        print ()

# main
print ("Print 0 blank line")
newline(0)
print ("Print 1 blank line")
newline(1)
print ("Print 2 blank lines")
newline(2)
print ("End")
```

Sample Output
```
Print 0 blank line
Print 1 blank line

Print 2 blank lines


End
```

Program 7.24 uses the modulus/remainder operator (%) to test if a number is odd or even.

Program 7.24
```
# tests if a number is even or odd
```

118

```
def evenodd(n):
    if n%2 == 0:
        return "even"
    else:
        return "odd"

while True:
    n = int(input("Enter an integer (0 to exit): "))
    if n==0:
        break
    else:
        print ("{0} is {1}".format(n, evenodd(n)))
print ("Done")
```

Sample Output
```
Enter an integer (0 to exit): 57
57 is odd

Enter an integer (0 to exit): 58
58 is even

Enter an integer (0 to exit): 130
130 is even

Enter an integer (0 to exit): 737
737 is odd

Enter an integer (0 to exit): 0
Done
```

Program 7.25 generates a 7-character password from a list of upper and lowercase letters, digits and special characters. It imports the random module and uses the randint method to generate a random number to select a character from the list.

Program 7.25
```
# imports random from system library
import random

# function to generate a 7 character password
def password():
    small = 'abcdefghijklmnopqrstuvwxyz'
    list1 = [i for i in small] # convert string to list
    caps = 'ABCDEFGHIJKLMNOPQRSTUVWXYZ'
    list2 = [i for i in caps]
    spec = '!@#$%^&=*+?()[]{}'
    list3 = [i for i in spec]
    mylist = list1 + list2 + list3
    n = len(mylist)
    pwd = ''
    for i in range(7):
        # generate random number between 0 and n-1
        pwd = pwd + mylist[random.randint(0, n-1)]
    return pwd

# main
k = int(input("Enter no. of passwords: "))
for i in range (0, k):
    pwd = password()
    print ("Password {0} is: {1}".format(i+1, pwd))
```

Sample Output
```
Enter no. of passwords: 5
```

```
Password 1 is: mh^YEm?
Password 2 is: ]cG(zt@
Password 3 is: LW#)SN(
Password 4 is: w#CN+cg
Password 5 is: UB&NX{%
```

Exercise

1. Given a list of integers. Write a function (max_min) to compute the maximum and minimum.

2. Given the principal (p), rate of interest (r) and number of years (n), write a function calculate the interest payable (i).

3. Given the coordinates of a triangle (x1, y1) , (x2, y2) , (x3, y3), write a function to calculate its area. (Hint: Area = x1*y2 + x2*y3 + x3*y1 - y1*x2 - y2*x3 - y3*x1)

4. Given a sentence up to 70 characters long, write functions to perform the following tasks:

   (a) Count the number of a in the sentence
   (b) Replace all e with E
   (c) Change all uppercase letters to lowercase and vice versa
   (d) Remove all embedded blank spaces.

   Repeat the above for 5 sentences.

5. Write a function to count the number of tokens in a string (e.g. the string "It is a gorgeous day" has 5 tokens. Test your code 5 strings.

6. Write a function to simulate a table-tennis game where one player has a 70 percent chance of winning each point.

7. Compute the factorial of n = 5 using (a) recursion and (b) without using recursion.

8. Write a function to generate n spaces for spacing for using in the print statement/function.

9. Write a program that calls the following functions:

   (a) ran() - to generate a n=100 integer random numbers between 100 and 999 in list x
   (b) even() - to count the number of even numbers in x
   (c) prime() – to count the number of prime numbers in x.

10. Create an anonymous/lambda function to find the hypotenuse of a right-angled triangle given the length of other two sides.

11. Trace the output for the code below:

```
def f():
    global s
    print (s)
    s = 'great men and women'
    print (s)

s = 'great boys and girls'
f()
print (s)
```

Chapter 8

Classes

Learning Outcomes:

After completing this chapter, the student will be able to

- *Define classes with their members.*
- *Create class objects.*
- *Distinguish between class variables and instance variables.*
- *Define base (parent or super) and derived (child or sub) classes.*
- *Explain class inheritance.*
- *Explain method overloading and overriding.*
- *Explain operator overloading.*
- *Explain object interaction.*
- *Write code for all the above.*

8.1 Object-oriented Concepts

A class bundle data (variables) and functionality (methods) together. Classes are the basic building blocks for object-oriented programming.

Object-oriented programming works something like this: First, you define a class with its members – variables and methods. Then you create objects (class instances) and manipulate the objects data using the methods defined in the class.

Let's illustrate with an example. Let's say a bank wants to create an account for its customer. To do that it can define an `Account` class with variables like `acct_no`, `name` and `balance` and methods like `openAccount`, `deposit`, `withdraw` and `showBalance`.

After it is defined, it can create `Account` objects and access its variables (`acct_no`, `name`, `balance`) using its class methods (`openAccount`, `deposit`, `withdraw`, `showBalance`) as follows:

```
a = Account()        # create an instance of Account
a.acct_no            # access variable acct_no
a.name
a.balance
a.openAccount()      # call openAccount method
a.deposit()
a.withdraw()
a.showBalance()
```

You need to be familiar with several object-oriented concepts. Here we list them briefly. They will become more clear as we go the various sections in this chapter.

- *Class* – a prototype that bundles attributes (data) and behaviors (methods).

- *Method* – a function defined within a class.

- *Class variable* – a static variable declared inside a class that is shared by *all* instances of that class.

- *Class instance* – an object created from a class. It has its own variables and can access all the methods in the class.

- *Instance variable* – a variable defined inside a class method that belongs only to that instance.

- *Data member* – a static variable in a class or an instance variable that holds the data associated with the class and its objects.

- *Inheritance* – a derived (subclass) class inheriting the attributes (variables) and behaviors (methods) of its base (parent) classes.

- *Method overloading* – two or more methods with the *same* name but with different number of parameters and/or parameter types.

- *Method overriding* – a derived class method that has the same name as base class method but has different functionality.

- *Operator overloading* – assigning more than one meaning to an operator.

8.2 Defining Classes

A class represents a person, item, place, event or concept. It bundles both attributes and functionality together. Attributes refer to variables and functionality refers to methods. The variables and methods are called members of the class.

A class is a template for creating objects. Objects are class instances. To illustrate, let's take the class Person with attributes like id, name and age and methods like displayInfo() and editInfo(). We can then create objects like Sam, Sally and Wong from the class Person. We can say Sam, Sally and Wong are objects of type Person.

Each object (class instance) has its unique variables and can access the methods in the class. While each object has its own variables, they all share the same methods. For example, Sam, Sally and Wong will have their own separate id, name and age, but they all share the same methods displayInfo() and editInfo().

A class definition in Python takes the form

```
class Class_name:
    class members    # class variables and methods
```

where class is a keyword, Class_name is the name of the class, and class members are its variables and methods.

Here are some examples of class definition.

Program 8.1 declares the class Circle with four methods:

The __init__(self, radius) method, also called *constructor*, creates (and initializes) instances of Circle. The instances are also called *objects*. The constructor has two parameters – self and radius. The *first* parameter self is always required – it points to current object (equivalent to *this* in C#). The second parameter radius is *input* to the constructor. The assignment self.radius = radius assigns the input to the instance variable radius (prefixed with self). Note that radius on the right-hand side is the input while the radius on the left-hand side is the instance variable. (The input doesn't have to have the same name, but by convention we use the same name.)

The area (self) method calculates and returns the area of the circle using the instance variable radius.

The circumference (self) method calculates and returns the circumference of the circle using the instance variable radius.

The display (self) method receives the inputs area and circumference and displays their values.

Note: *Instance variables* must always be prefixed with self.

Program 8.1
```
# defines class Circle

class Circle:

# constructor
   def __init__(self, radius): # radius is input
       self.radius = radius

# computes area
   def area(self):
       return 3.14 * self.radius**2   # return area

# computes circumference
   def circumference(self):
       return 2 * 3.14 * self.radius # return circumference

# displays area and circumference
   def display(self, area, circum):
       print ('Radius = %7.2f' % radius)
       print ('Area = %7.2f' % area)
       print ('Circumference = %7.2f' % circum)

# main function
radius = 5.86
cir = Circle(radius)   # create an object
area = cir.area()      # call area method
circum = cir.circumference()   # call circumference method
cir.display(area, circum)      # call display method
```

Output
```
Radius =     5.86
Area =   107.83
Circumference =    36.80
```

Program 8.2 produces the same result as Program 8.1, but is more compact. It combines the area () and circumference () methods into one - areacircum () - and returns area and circumference.

Program 8.2
```
class Circle:

   def __init__(self, radius):
       self.radius = radius

   def areacircum(self):
       area = 3.14 * self.radius**2
       circum = 2 * 3.14 * self.radius
       return area, circum   # returns 2 values

   def display(self, area, circum):
       print ('Radius = %7.2f' % radius)
```

124

```
        print ('Area = %7.2f' % area)
        print ('Circumference = %7.2f' % circum)

# main function
radius  = 5.86
cir = Circle(radius)
area, circum = cir.areacircum() # receives 2 values from functions
cir.display(area, circum)
```

Output
```
Radius =    5.86
Area =   107.83
Circumference =    36.80
```

Program 8.3 has a class (Account) and one static variable (bank) and four methods (__init__(), deposit(), withdraw(), displayAccount()). The __init__() method is a special method used to initialize objects when they are created. It is called a *constructor*. The main function creates two instances of Account()- a1 and a2 - and calls the methods deposit(), widthdraw() and displayAccount().

The constructor __init__() has a special parameter called *self* which is used to reference the current instance. To access instance variables, you must prefix them with *self*. Thus you use self.balance to access balance.

The variable bank is a *class* variable, not an instance variable. It is attached to the class, *not* to a class instance. It's a *static* variable shared by all instances. Python maintains only *one* copy for all class instances.

Note: *Class variables* must always be prefixed with the class name.

Program 8.3
```
# class definition
class Account:
    bank = 'My Community Bank'  # class variable

    def __init__(self, acct, name, balance): # constructor
        self.acct = acct  # acct is an instance variable
        self.name = name
        self.balance = balance

    def deposit(self, acct, amount):
        self.balance = self.balance + amount

    def withdraw(self, acct, amount):
        self.balance = self.balance - amount

    def display(self, acct):
        print ('Account No: {}\t\tName: {}\tBalance: ${:.2f}'.format\
               (acct, self.name, self.balance))

# main function
print (Account.bank)  # print bank name; bank is a class variable

n = 2
a = [' ', ' ', 0,]*2
for i in range(n):
    a[i] = Account('111', 'Joe', 1000.0) # create a1 of type Account
    a[i] = Account('222', 'Sam', 2000.0) # create another

a[0].deposit('222', 700)
a[0].withdraw('222', 300)
a[0].display('222')
```

125

```
a[1].deposit('111', 500)   # a1 calls deposit method
a[1].withdraw('111', 200)
a[1].display('111')
```

Output
```
My Community Bank
Account No: 222        Name: Sam      Balance: $2400.00
Account No: 111        Name: Sam      Balance: $2300.00
```

Creating a class instance takes the form

```
var = Class_name()
```

The above program creates two `Account` instances as follows:

```
a1 = Account()   # create an instance of Account
a2 = Account()
```

To access the class variable `bank`, you prefix it with the class name as follows:

```
Account.bank
```

8.3 Class Inheritance

In Python, you can create a hierarchy of classes consisting of a base (or super) class and one or more derived (or sub) classes. For example, you can create a class hierarchy as shown below. Here, Shape is a base class, and `Circle` and `Triangle` are derived classes (derived from `Shape`).

Shape — base/super class

Circle   Triangle — derived/sub class (derived from Shape)

A derived class automatically inherits the variables (attributes) and methods (behaviors) of the base class. That means a derived class can use variables and methods defined in the base class. The derived classes only need to include additional variables and methods that they need. (This promotes software reuse as derived classes can use all the attributes and methods of the base class.)

The base class defines *general* attributes and behaviors while the derived classes define *specific* attributes and behaviors.

For the above example, the code for class hierarchy takes the form

```
class Shape:   # base class
    Shape members   # attributes and methods

class Circle(Shape):   # derived class
    Circle members
class Triangle(Shape): # derived class
    Triangle members
```

Program 8.4 illustrates class inheritance. It has a base class - Shape - and a derived class - Circle. Each class has a constructor and another function. It creates an object s from Shape and an object c from Circle. Each object calls its own class method.

Program 8.4
```
# example of class inheritance

# define Shape class
class Shape:          # base class

    def __init__(self):
        print ("Calling Shape constructor")

    def shapeMethod(self):
        print ('Calling Shape method')

# define Circle class
class Circle(Shape): # derived class

    def __init__(self):
        print ("Calling Circle constructor")

    def circleMethod(self):
        print ('Calling Circle method')

# main
s = Shape()            # create a Shape object
s.shapeMethod()        # calls its method
c = Circle()           # create a Circle object
c.circleMethod()       # calls its method
```

Output
```
Calling Shape constructor
Calling Shape method
Calling Circle constructor
Calling Circle method
```

Program 8.5 is another example of class inheritance. It has two derived classes: Circle and Triangle.

The class Shape has two methods: __init__() and display(). The constructor has no parameters. The keyword pass in the constructor tells that it has no attributes. The display() method displays the values of name and area passed to it.

The class Circle(Shape) – derived from Shape – has two methods: __init__() and area(). The constructor has the attribute radius. The area() method calculates the area of a circle using the attribute radius.

The class Triangle(Shape) is similar. The constructor has two attributes: base and height. The area() method calculates the area given the base and height.

Program 8.5
```
# example of class inheritance

class Shape:
    def __init__(self):
        pass  # do nothing

    def display(self, name, area):
        print ('Area of %6s = %7.2f' % (name, area))
```

```
class Circle(Shape):    # derived from Shape

    def __init__(self, radius):
        self.radius = radius

    def area(self):
        area = 3.14 * self.radius**2
        return area

class Triangle(Shape):   # derived from Shape
    def __init__(self, base, height):
        self.base = base
        self.height = height

    def area(self):
        area = 0.5 * self.base * self.height
        return area

# main
c = Circle(2.8)   # create a Circle object
t = Triangle(5.4, 6.2)   # create a Triangle object
cirarea = c.area() # call the Circle area method
triarea = t.area()
Shape().display('circle', cirarea) # call Shape display method
Shape().display('triangle', triarea)
```

Output
```
Area of circle =    24.62
Area of triangle =    16.74
```

The diagram below illustrates a three-level class hierarchy:

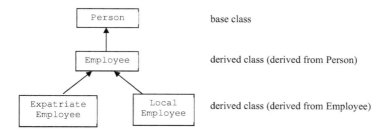

Here, `Person` is the base class; `Employee` is a derived class (derived from `Person`); and `Expatriate Employee` and `Local Employee` classes are derived classes (derived from `Employee`).

Note that Employee is both a derived class (derived from Person) and a base class (for classes Expatriate Employee and Local Employee).

The code for this takes the form:

```
class Person:
    #Person class members

class Employee(Person):   # derived from Person
```

128

```
#Employee class members

class ExpatriateEmployee(Employee): # derived from Employee
    #ExpatriateEmployee class members

class LocalEmployee(Employee):
    # LocalEmployee class members
```

Python allows a class to inherit from multiple classes as shown in the diagram below. Here, the class StudentWorker inherits all the attributes and methods of the Employee and Student classes.

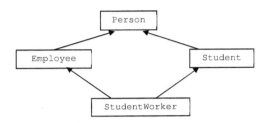

The code for the above class hierarch takes the form:

```
class Person:
    # Person class members

class Employee(Person):  # inherits from Person class
    # Employee class members

class StudentWorker(Student, Employee): #inherits from Student and Employee
    # StudentWorker class members
```

Program 8.6 is an example of class inheritance. PartEmp is derived from FullEmp. Note that printSalary() method appears in both classes, but the derived class *overrides* the method and thus stops the inheritance.

Program 8.6
```
# define FullEmp class
class FullEmp:          # base class
    salary = 0.0

    def __init__(self, basic, allowance):
        self.basic = basic
        self.allowance = allowance

    def printSalary(self):
        FullEmp.salary = self.basic + self.allowance
        print ('Salary of full-time employee: RM{:.2f}'.format\
            (FullEmp.salary))

# define PartEmp class
class PartEmp(FullEmp):  # derived class
    salary = 0.0

    def __init__(self, hours, rate):
        self.hours = hours
        self.rate = rate
```

129

```
    def printSalary(self): # overrides base class method
        PartEmp.salary = self.hours * self.rate
        print ('Salary of part-time employee: RM{:.2f}'.format\
            (PartEmp.salary))

# main
f = FullEmp(3000.00, 500.00)      # create FullEmp object
f.printSalary()                    # calls its method
p = PartEmp(35, 45.50)            # create PartEmp object
p.printSalary()                    # calls its method
```

Output
```
Salary of full-time employee: RM3500.00
Salary of part-time employee: RM1592.50
```

Program 8.7 has a base class - `FullEmp` - and a derived class - `PartEmp`. The base class has three methods – constructor, `printFullSalaray()` and `printHeading()`.The derived class has two methods – constructor and `printPartSalaray()`. It also inherits `printHeading()` from the base class.

Program 8.7
```
# define FullEmp class
class FullEmp:         # base class
    salary = 0.0

    def __init__(self, name, basic, allowance):
        self.name = name
        self.basic = basic
        self.allowance = allowance

    def printFullsalary(self):
        FullEmp.salary = self.basic + self.allowance
        print ('Salary of {:<10}: RM{:.2f}'.format(self.name, \
            FullEmp.salary))

    def printHeading(self, heading):
        self.heading = heading
        print (self.heading)

# define PartEmp class derived from FullEmp class
class PartEmp(FullEmp):      # derived class
    salary = 0.0

    def __init__(self, name, hours, rate):
        self.name = name
        self.hours = hours
        self.rate = rate

    def printPartsalary(self):
        PartEmp.salary = self.hours * self.rate
        print ('Salary of {:<8}: RM{:.2f}'.format \
            (self.name, PartEmp.salary))
# main
f = FullEmp('Sally', 3000.00, 500.00)
f.printHeading('Full-time Employee:')
f.printFullsalary()
print ()
p = PartEmp('John', 35, 45.50)
p.printHeading('Part-time Employee:')  # base class method
p.printPartsalary()
```

Output
```
Full-time Employee:
```

130

```
Salary of Sally     : RM3500.00

Part-time Employee:
Salary of John      : RM1592.50
```

8.4 Abstract Classes

Python doesn't define abstract classes like some other programming languages. Abstract classes declare abstract methods but they don't implement them. Abstract classes *cannot* be instantiated. The derived classes must implement the methods in the abstract class. Abstract classes are useful when you need to declare higher-level functions in the base class and implement them in the derived classes. In Python, subclasses are *not* required to implement abstract methods.

Program 8.8 illustrates abstract classes. `Account` is the abstract class and `Current` is the derived class. `Account` declares several functions which `Current` implements.

Program 8.8
```
# abstract class - cannot be instantiated
class Account:

    def show_bal(self, acct):
        pass

    def deposit(self, acct):
        pass

    def withdraw(self, acct):
        pass

# this derived class implements the above
class Current(Account):

    def __init__(self, acct, name, bal):
#       Account.__init__(self, acct, name, bal)
        self.acct = acct
        self.name = name
        self.bal = bal

    def show_bal(self, acct):
        print ('Account. No:', self.acct, '\tName: ', \
                self.name, '\tBalance: ', self.bal)

    def deposit(self, acct, amount):
        if acct == self.acct:
            self.bal += amount
        else:
            print ('Sorry, invalid account!')

    def withdraw(self, acct, amount):
        if acct == self.acct:
            if self.bal < amount:
                print('\nWithdrawal denied - insufficient fund \
                      in account!')
                print ('Balance:', self.bal, '\t\tWithdrawal request:', \
                      amount)
            else:
                self.bal -= amount
                return
        else:
            print ('Sorry, invalid account!')
# main
```

```
c1 = Current('111', 'Joe', 1000)
c1.deposit('111', 500)
c1.withdraw('111', 50)
c1.show_bal('111')
c1.withdraw('111', 700)
c1.deposit('111', 900)
c1.show_bal('111')
```

Output
```
Account No: 111    Name:  Joe     Balance:  1450
Account No: 111    Name:  Joe     Balance:  1650
```

8.5 Overloading & Overriding Methods

A method is said to be *overloaded* if two or more methods have the *same* name but performs different things. Overloaded methods have different number and/or parameter types.

Method overloading in Python works slightly differently from other languages. The special parameter *args (a tuple) specifies the parameter list, which can be zero or more (* means zero or more).

Program 8.9 illustrates method overloading. The variable count counts the number of parameters in *args. The if...elif...else statement then calls the appropriate print() method based on the number of parameters.

Program 8.9
```
class Fn_overload():
    def print_all(self, *args):
        count = len(args)
        if count == 0:
            print (args)
        elif count == 1:
            print (args[0:1])
        elif count == 2:
            print (args[0:2])
        elif count == 3:
            print (args[0:3])
        else:
            print (args[0:4])

fn = Fn_overload()   # creates an object
fn.print_all()         # calls the function; passes 0 parameter
fn.print_all('joe')    # calls the function; passes 1 parameter
fn.print_all('joe', 25)
fn.print_all('joe', 25, 70.5)
fn.print_all('joe', 25, 70.5, True)
```

Output
```
()
('joe',)
('joe', 25)
('joe', 25, 70.5)
('joe', 25, 70.5, True)
```
A method is said to be *polymorphic* (taking different forms) if it has the same name in the base and derived classes but they behave differently. In this case, we say the subclass method *overrides* the base class method.

Program 8.10 illustrates polymorphism. It uses two classes: A and B (derived from A). A has two functions - fn1() and fn2() - and B has one function - fn1(). The fn1 in B *overrides* the fn1 in A and thus it is not the same as the one in A. Note that the method b.print_fn2() calls the base class method fn2().

132

Program 8.10
```
# method overloading in class
class A:

    def print_fn1(self):
        print ('Printing from fn1 in class A')

    def print_fn2(self):
        print ('Printing from fn2 in class A')

class B(A):

    def print_fn1(self):
        print ('Printing from fn1 in class B')

a = A()  # create an object of type A (base class)
a.print_fn1()
a.print_fn2()

# same effect as the above
A().print_fn1()
A().print_fn2()

print ()
b = B()  # create an object of type B (derived class)
b.print_fn1()  # prints B class fn2
b.print_fn2()  # prints A class fn2
```

Output
```
Printing from fn1 in class A
Printing from fn2 in class A
Printing from fn1 in class A
Printing from fn2 in class A

Printing from fn1 in class B
Printing from fn2 in class A
```

Program 8.11 illustrates a three-level class hierarchy. Here, C inherits from B, and B inherits from A.

Program 8.11
```
# illustrates a 3-class hierarchy

class A: # base class
    ca = 'I am Class A variable'

    def print_fna(self):
        print ('I am class A function')

class B(A):  # derived from A
    cb = 'I am Class B variable'

    def print_fnb(self):
        print ('I am class B function')

class C(B): # derived from B
    cc = 'I am Class C variable'

    def print_fnc(self):
        print ('I am class C function')

a = A()  # base class
b = B()  # derived from class A
c = C()  # derived from class B
```

```
# calling functions from class instances
a.print_fna()
b.print_fnb()
c.print_fnc()

print ('\nSame as above.')
# calling functions from classes
A().print_fna()
B().print_fnb()
C().print_fnc()

# accessing variables from class instances
print('\nAccessing variables from classes A, B and C.')
print (a.ca)
print (b.cb)
print (c.cc)
print ('\nSame as above.')

# accessing variables from classes
print (A().ca)
print (B().cb)
print (C().cc)

# calling base class functions
print('\nCalling class A function from class B: ')
b.print_fna()

# calling class B function from C
print('\nCalling class B function from class C: ')
c.print_fnb()

# accessing class A and B variables from C
print('\nAccessing class A and B variables from class C: ')
print ('From C accessing A variable: ', c.ca)
print ('From C accessing B variable: ', c.cb)
```

Output

```
I am class A function
I am class B function
I am class C function

Same as above.
I am class A function
I am class B function
I am class C function

Accessing variables from classes A, B and C.
I am Class A variable
I am Class B variable
I am Class C variable

Same as above.
I am Class A variable
I am Class B variable
I am Class C variable

Calling class A function from class B:
I am class A function

Calling class B function from class C:
I am class B function

Accessing class A and B variables from class C:
```

From C accessing A variable: I am Class A variable
From C accessing B variable: I am Class B variable

8.6 Operator Overloading

An operator is said to be overloaded when it does more than one operation.

Program 8.12 illustrates overloads the + operator. It does vector addition - adds the corresponding items in two vectors.

Program 8.12
```
# overloading the + operator

class Vector:
    def __init__(self, x, y): # constructor
        self.x = x
        self.y = y

    def __str__(self):
        # return result vector
        return 'Vector: ({}, {})'.format(self.x, self.y)

    def __add__(self, vec):
        # create an instance of Vector
        v = Vector(self.x + vec.x, self.y + vec.y)
        return v

# main
v1 = Vector(1, 2)
v2 = Vector(11, 22)
print (v1 + v2)
```

Output
```
Vector: (12, 24)
```

Program 8.13 does the same for subtraction.

Program 8.13
```
# overloading the - operator
class Vector:
    def __init__(self, x, y): # constructor
        self.x = x
        self.y = y

    def __str__(self):
        # return result vector
        return 'Vector: ({}, {})'.format(self.x, self.y)

    def __sub__(self, vec):
        # create an instance of Vector
        v = Vector(self.x - vec.x, self.y - vec.y)
        return v

# main
v1 = Vector(1, 2)
v2 = Vector(11, 22)
print (v1 - v2)
```

Output
```
Vector: (-10, -20)
```

135

8.7 Object Interaction

A typical application will have several class objects, each with its own attributes and methods. Each object encapsulates all the attributes and methods it requires.

Objects in a system interact with one another to perform the needed business tasks. They interact by passing messages to one another and requesting them to perform certain tasks. Message passing is similar to calling a function.

Program 8.14 illustrates object interaction. It defines two classes - Product and Order - each with its own attributes and methods. The main function creates an Order object called ord. The ord object then creates an Inventory object called inv and sends messages to inv to fetch the product prod_price and prod_name. Using these objects it processes the transaction.

Program 8.14
```
# illustrates object interaction

class Product:
    prod_id = [1, 2, 3, 4, 5]
    prod_name = ['Pen', 'Mouse', 'USB Cable', 'Pendrive', 'Jacket']
    prod_price = [15.00, 22.90, 14.60, 25.50, 15.90]
    n = len(prod_id)

    def get_price(self, id):
        for i in range(Product.n):
            if id == Product.prod_id[i]:
                price = Product.prod_price[i]
                return price

    def get_name(self, id):
        for i in range (Product.n):
            if id == Product.prod_id[i]:
                name = Product.prod_name[i]
                return name

class Order:
    price = 0
    amount = 0
    pid = 0
    pname = ''
    qty = 0
    match = False

    def get_data(self):
        Order.pid = int(input('Enter product id (0-4): '))
        for i in range(Product.n):
            if Order.pid == Product.prod_id[i]:
                Order.qty = int(input('Enter quantity: '))
                Order.pname = Product.prod_name[i]
                Order.price = Product.prod_price[i]
                Order.match = True

    def get_info(self):
        if Order.match:
            prod = Product()   # create an instance of Product
            prod.get_price(Order.pid)
            prod.get_name(Order.pname)

    def compute(self):
```

136

```
            Order.amount = Order.qty * Order.price;

    def gen_report(self):
        print ('\nProduct id: ', Order.pid)
        print ('Product name: ', Order.pname)
        print ('Quantity: ', Order.qty)
        print ('Unit price: {:.2f}'.format(Order.price))
        print ('Amount: {:.2f}'.format(Order.amount))

# main
ord = Order()
ord.get_data()
ord.get_info()
if Order.match:
    ord.compute()
    ord.gen_report()
```

Output
```
Enter product id (0-4): 4

Enter quantity: 3

Product id:   4
Product name:   Pendrive
Quantity:    3
Unit price: 25.50
Amount: 76.50
```

8.8 Sample Programs

This section gives additional examples using classes.

Program 8.15 defines the Employee class with class variable count and instance variables name and salary and class methods __init__() and dispayEmployee(). The main function creates two Employee objects and calls these methods to display their name and salary.

Program 8.15
```
# class definition
class Employee:
    count = 0  # class variable

    def __init__(self, name, salary): # function definition in class
        self.name = name  # instance variable
        self.salary = salary

    def displayEmployee(self):
        print ('Name: {0}\tSalary: {1}'.format(self.name,self.salary))
        Employee.count += 1  # increment class vaiable
# main
emp1 = Employee('Johnson', 5000) # create employee object
emp2 = Employee('Jennifer', 4500)
emp1.displayEmployee()  # call method/function
emp2.displayEmployee()
print ('No. of employees:', Employee.count)
```

Output
```
Name: Johnson     Salary: 5000
Name: Jennifer    Salary: 4500
No. of employees: 2
```

Program 8.16 is similar to the above but adds more details. It calculates `salary`, given `basic`, `overtime hours` and `rate`. It also calculates `total` and `average` salary.

Program 8.16
```
# class definition
class Employee:
    total = 0
    average = 0

    def __init__(self, id, name, basic, hours, rate):
        self.id = id
        self.name = name
        self.basic = basic
        self.hours = hours
        self.rate = rate

    def computesalary(self):
        salary = self.basic + self. hours * self.rate
        Employee.total = Employee.total + salary
        return salary

    def display(self, count, salary):
        print ('%2d %4s %4s %8.2f %8.2f %8.2f %9.2f' % (count, \
          self.id, self.name,self.basic, self.hours, self.rate, salary))

# main
# process exam results

f = open(r'C:\Users\sell780\Desktop\employee.txt')
print ('No. Id    Name    Basic(RM)  Hours    Rate(RM) Salary(RM)')

count = 0
for line in f:
    line = line.rstrip('\n')
    rec = line.split(',')
    e = Employee(rec[0], rec[1], float(rec[2]), float(rec[3]), \
                 float(rec[4]))          count = count + 1
    salary = e.computesalary()
    e.display(count, salary)
f.close()
print ('\n  Total salary = RM%7.2f' % Employee.total)
print ('  Average salary = RM%7.2f' % (Employee.total/count))
```

Output
```
No. Id    Name    Basic(RM)  Hours    Rate(RM) Salary(RM)
 1  111   sally   2700.00    10.00    40.00    3100.00
 2  222   chong   2800.00    16.00    42.00    3472.00
 3  333   sammy   2000.00    10.00    50.00    2500.00
 4  444   megan   2600.00    12.00    45.00    3140.00
 5  555   leong   3500.00    16.00    55.00    4380.00

Total salary = RM16592.00
Average salary = RM3318.40
```

Program 8.17 defines the class `Robot` and creates two instances of `Robot`, namely, `r1` and `r2` and then displays their information.

Program 8.17
```
# defining class
class Robot:

    def __init__(self, name, color, wt):
```

138

```
        self.name = name
        self.color = color
        self.wt = wt

    def display(self):
        print ('%7s  %6s  %6d' % (self.name, self.color, self.wt))

# main
r1 = Robot('musician ', 'yellow', 50)
r2 = Robot('performer', 'purple', 40)

print('Name        Color      Weight')
r1.display()
r2.display()
```

Output
```
Name        Color      Weight
musician    yellow        50
performer   purple        40
```

Program 8.18 defines the `Student` class with class variable `count` and instance variables `name` and `mark` and class methods `__init__()`, `computeGrade()` and `dispayResult()`. The `main` function creates two `Student` objects and calls these methods to compute and display their grades.

Program 8.18
```
# class definition
class Student:
    count = 0   # class variable

    def __init__(self, name, mark):
        self.name = name   # instance variable
        self.mark = mark
        self.grade = ' '

    def computeGrade(self):
        if self.mark < 50:
            self.grade = 'Fail'
        else:
            self.grade = 'Pass'

    def displayResult(self):
        print ('Name: {0}\tMark: {1}\t Grade: {2}'.format\
                (self.name,self.mark, self.grade))
        Student.count += 1   # increment class variable

# main
stud1 = Student('Johnson', 49) # create student object
stud1.computeGrade()   # call method
stud1.displayResult()
stud2 = Student('Jennifer', 65)
stud2.computeGrade()
stud2.displayResult()
print ('No. of students:', Student.count)
```

Output
```
Name: Johnson    Mark: 49  Grade: Fail
Name: Jennifer   Mark: 65  Grade: Pass
No. of students: 2
```

Program 8.19 uses class variables `slist` and `mlist` and instance variables `name` and `mark` and class methods `__init__()`, `computeGrade()` and `dispayResult()`. The `main` function creates a

139

Student object and calls these methods to compute and display their grades. It iterates for all the students in the list.

Program 8.19
```
# class definition
class Student:
    slist = ['Sam', 'Joe', 'May']   # class list
    mlist = [77, 45, 98]
    n = len(slist)   # get length of list

    def __init__(self, name, mark):
        self.name = name
        self.mark = mark
        self.grade = ''

    def computeGrade(self):
        if self.mark < 50:
            self.grade = 'Fail'
        else:
            self.grade = 'Pass'

    def displayResult(self, i):
        print ('{0}\t{1}\t{2}\t{3}'.format(i+1, self.name, \
                self.mark, self.grade))

# main
print ('No.\tName\tMark\tGrade')   # print heading
# process all the items in the list
for i in range (Student.n):
    stud = Student(Student.slist[i], Student.mlist[i])
    stud.computeGrade()
    stud.displayResult(i)
print ('\nNo. of students:', Student.n)
```

Output
```
No.     Name    Mark    Grade
1       Sam     77      Pass
2       Joe     45      Fail
3       May     98      Pass

No. of students: 3
```

Program 8.20 reads student details – name, coursework, midterm and final marks - from text file mark , then computes and prints the grade.

Program 8.20
```
# class definition
class Student:
    def __init__(self, name, cw, midterm, final):
        self.name = name
        self.cw = cw
        self.midterm = midterm
        self.final = final
        self.total = 0
        self.grade = ''

    def computeGrade(self):
        self.total = self.cw + self.midterm + self.final
        if self.total < 50:
            self.grade = 'Fail'
        else:
            self.grade = 'Pass'
```

```
    def displayResult(self, n):
        print ('{:^3} {:<10} {:^5} {:^10} {:^6} {:^6} {:^5}'.format(n,\
                self.name, self.cw,self.midterm, self.final, \
                self.total, self.grade))

# main
print ('No. Name        Course  Midterm   Final Total  Grade')
# open file to read input data
# the prefix r specifies raw data to avoid Unicode character \U
f = open(r'C:\Users\sell780\Desktop\mark.txt')
n = 0
for line in f:
    line = line.rstrip('\n')
    rec = line.split(',')
    stud = Student(rec[0], int(rec[1]), int(rec[2]), int(rec[3]))
    stud.computeGrade()
    stud.displayResult(n+1)
    n = n + 1
f.close()
```

Output

No.	Name	Course	Midterm	Final	Total	Grade
1	John	25	15	40	80	Pass
2	Sally	24	17	38	79	Pass
3	Wong	28	18	42	88	Pass
4	Kumar	25	16	40	81	Pass
5	Peter	20	10	10	40	Fail

Program 8.21 has two classes: `Circle` and `Triangle`. The `Circle` class uses the parameter `radius` to compute and print its area and circumference; and the `Triangle` class uses the parameters `base` and `height` to compute and print its area.

Program 8.21

```
class Circle:

    def __init__(self, radius):
        self.radius = radius
        self.area = 0
        self.circumference = 0

    def circleArea(self):
        self.area = 3.14 * self.radius**2

    def circleCircumference(self):
        self.circumference = 2 * 3.14 * self.radius

    def printCircleinfo(self):
        print ('Area of circle with radius {:.2f} = {:.2f}'.format \
                (self.radius, self.area))
        print ('Circumference of circle with radius {:.2f}: {:.2f} = '. \
                format(self.radius, self.circumference))

class Triangle:

    def __init__(self, base, height):
        self.base = base
        self.height = height
        self.area = 0

    def triangleArea(self):
        self.area = 0.5 * self.base * self.height
```

```
    def printTriangleinfo(self):
        print ('Area of triangle with base {:.2f} and height {:.2f} = \
                {:.2f}'.format (self.base, self.height, self.area))

# main

radius  = 5.8
cir = Circle(radius)
cir.circleArea()
cir.circleCircumference()
cir.printCircleinfo()

base = 4.6
height = 3.2
tri = Triangle(base, height)
tri.triangleArea()
tri.printTriangleinfo()
```

Output
```
Area of circle with radius 5.80 = 105.63
Circumference of circle with radius 5.80: 36.42 =
Area of triangle with base 4.60 and height 3.20 = 7.36
```

Program 8.22 has three classes: base class `Account` and derived classes `Current` and `Saving`. `Account` has two attributes - `acct` (account number) and `name` (account name). `Current` has one attribute - `curbal` (current balance) - in addition to the two derived attributes `acct` and `name`. Similarly, `Saving` has one attribute - `savbal` (saving balance) - in addition to the two derived attributes `acct` and `name`.

The program creates two instances of `Account` (`a1`, `a2`), and two instances of `Current` (`c1`, `c2`) and two instances of `Saving` (`s1`, `s2`) with some initial deposits. Then it shows deposit and withdraw transactions for the `Current` and `Saving` accounts.

Program 8.22
```
# class inheritance
# base class Account; derived classes Current and Saving

class Account:

    bank = 'My Community Bank'

    def __init__(self, acct, name):
        self.acct = acct
        self.name = name

    def showAccount(self, acct):
        if acct == self.acct:
            print ('Account No:', self.acct, '\tName:', self.name)
        else:
            print ('Sorry, invalid account!')

    def showbal(self, acct, name, accttype, trans, amount, newbal):
        print ()
        print ('Account No: {0}\t\tName: {1}\t\tAccount Type: {2} \
                \n{3}{4}\t\tNew Balance: {5}'.format(acct, \
                name, accttype, trans, amount, newbal))

    def open_acct(self, acct, name, accttype, amount):
        print ()
        print ('Account No: {}\t\tName: {}\t\tAccount Type: {} \
                \nOpening Balance: {}'.format(acct, name, accttype, amount))
```

142

```python
class Current(Account):

    def __init__(self, acct, name, curbal):
        Account.__init__(self, acct, name)
        self.curbal = curbal
        super().open_acct(acct, name, 'Current', self.curbal)

    def deposit(self, acct, amount):
        if acct == self.acct:
            self.curbal += amount
            super().showbal(acct, self.name, 'Current', \
                    'Deposit: ', amount, self.curbal)
        else:
            print ('Sorry, invalid account!')

    def withdraw(self, acct, amount):
        if acct == self.acct:
            if self.curbal < amount:
                print('\nWithdrawal denied - insufficient fund in \
                    Current account!')
                print ('Balance:', self.curbal, '\t\tWithdrawal \
                    request:', amount)
            else:
                self.curbal -= amount
                super().showbal(acct, self.name, 'Current', \
                        'Withdrawal: ', amount, self.curbal)
            return
        else:
            print ('Sorry, invalid account!')

class Saving(Account):

    def __init__(self, acct, name, savbal):
        Account.__init__(self, acct, name)
        self.savbal = savbal
        super().open_acct(acct, name, 'Saving', self.savbal)

    def deposit(self, acct, amount):
        if acct == self.acct:
            self.savbal += amount
            super().showbal(acct, self.name, 'Saving', 'Deposit: ', \
            amount, self.savbal)
        else:
            print ('Sorry, invalid account!')

    def withdraw(self, acct, amount):
        if acct == self.acct:
            if self.savbal < amount:
                print('\nWithdrawal denied - insufficient fund in \
                    Saving account!')
                print ('Balance:', self.savbal, '\t\tWithdrawal \
                    request:', amount)
            else:
                self.savbal -= amount
                super().showbal(acct, self.name, 'Saving', \
                'Withdrawal: ', amount, self.savbal)
            return
        else:
            print ('Sorry, invalid account!')

# main
print (Account.bank, '\n')
a1 = Account('111', 'Joe')
```

```
a1.showAccount('111')

c1 = Current('111', 'Joe', 1000)
c1.deposit('111', 500)
c1.withdraw('111', 50)

s1 = Saving('111', 'Joe', 2000)
s1.deposit('111', 200)
s1.withdraw('111', 20)
print ()
a2 = Account('222', 'Sally')
a2.showAccount('222')

c2 = Current('222', 'Sally', 3000)
c2.deposit('222', 300)
c2.withdraw('222', 4000)

s2 = Saving('222', 'Sally', 4000)
s2.deposit('222', 400)
s2.withdraw('222', 5000)
```

Output
```
My Community Bank

Account No: 111          Name: Joe

Account No: 111          Name: Joe              Account Type: Current
Opening Balance: 1000

Account No: 111          Name: Joe              Account Type: Current
Deposit: 500             New Balance: 1500

Account No: 111          Name: Joe              Account Type: Current
Withdrawal: 50           New Balance: 1450

Account No: 111          Name: Joe              Account Type: Saving
Opening Balance: 2000

Account No: 111          Name: Joe              Account Type: Saving
Deposit: 200             New Balance: 2200

Account No: 111          Name: Joe              Account Type: Saving
Withdrawal: 20           New Balance: 2180

Account No: 222          Name: Sally

Account No: 222          Name: Sally            Account Type: Current
Opening Balance: 3000

Account No: 222          Name: Sally            Account Type: Current
Deposit: 300             New Balance: 3300

Withdrawal denied - insufficient fund in Current account!
Balance: 3300            Withdrawal request: 4000

Account No: 222          Name: Sally            Account Type: Saving
Opening Balance: 4000

Account No: 222          Name: Sally            Account Type: Saving
Deposit: 400             New Balance: 4400

Withdrawal denied - insufficient fund in Saving account!
Balance: 4400            Withdrawal request: 5000
```

Exercise

1. Write a program to implement the class `Student` with the following attributes and methods:

   Attributes
   stud_id   - string
   stud_name - string
   mark - integer

   Methods
   get_data()   - to get data from keyboard for stud_id, stud_name and mark
   compute_grade()   - to compute the grade (A:80-100, B:60-79, C: 50-59, F: 0-49)
   display_grade()   - to display stud_id, stud_name, mark and grade

2. Do question 1 for n=5 students. Also calculate and display the average.

3. Write a program to create and implement the class `Employee`, which will have the following attributes and methods:

   Attributes
   emp_id   - string
   emp_name - string
   hours_worked   - double
   rate - static double (fixed at 25.00)

   Methods
   get_data()   - to get data from keyboard for emp_id, emp_name and hours_worked
   compute_salary()   - to compute salary (salary = hours_worked * rate)
   display_grade()   - to display emp_id, emp_name, hours_worked and salary

4. Do question 3 for n=7 employees. The salary is now calculated as follows: For the first 40 hours worked, the rate is as given and for the remaining hours the rate is twice that amount.

5. Define `Shape` as base class and `Triangle` and `Circle` as derived classes with the following attributes and methods:

   Shape

   Triangle
   Attributes - base and height
   Method - area()

   Circle
   attributes - radius
   methods - area() and circumference()

6. Distinguish between static and instance variables. Write code to show the difference between the two.

7. What is (a) an abstract class (b) an abstract method? Write a program to illustrate these concepts.

8. What is polymorphism? What purpose does it serve? Write code to illustrate the concept of polymorphism.

9. Write a program using three classes – registration, course and student – that will interact with one another such that the registration object will retrieve information from the Course and Student objects and display all the attributes. The attributes for the classes are as follows:

Registration
```
stud_id - string
course_code - string
stud_name - string
course_name - string
```

Course
course_code – string
course_name – string
credits – integer

Student
stud_id – string
stud_name – string
email – string

10. Write a program to compute the area of a polygon given the number of sides using the base class `Shape` and the derived class `Polygon`.

Chapter 9

Threading

Learning Outcomes:

After completing this chapter, the student will be able to

- *Explain what threads are.*
- *Explain thread methods.*
- *Create, start and run threads.*
- *Create multiple threads.*
- *Synchronize threads.*
- *Access shared resources.*

9.1 What are Threads?

A thread, also known as a *lightweight process*, is a unit of execution sequence *within* a process. Threads don't have a separate existence – they exist only within a process. All the threads spawned by a process share the same resources. This making threads lightweight in terms of processing overheads.

A process can spawn multiple threads, each running independently. But they can also communicate with each other as when necessary. For example, a thread may send a message to another thread and wait for that thread to send an acknowledgement before continuing its execution. Threads can also be used to control access to shared resources where only one thread should have has access at any given time.

A thread has a beginning, an execution phase, and an end. A thread can be in one of several states such as running, waiting, sleeping, or alive. A thread may be preempted, interrupted or suspended and later awakened or resumed. However, at any given point in time, the thread has only a single point of execution. It has an instruction pointer that keeps track of where in its context it is currently running.

9.2 Importing Threading Module

To use threads, you need to import the threading module as follows:

```
import threading
```

Or you can specifically import the `Thread` class from the threading module as follows:

```
from threading import Thread
```

Once imported, you can start creating threads.

There are two ways of creating threads: using functions or using classes. We will look at both in the sequel.

147

9.3 Thread Methods

The threading module has many thread classes, each with its own methods.

The table below gives a list of these methods.

Thread method	Description
active_count()	Returns the number of Thread objects currently alive. The returned count is equal to the length of the list returned by enumerate().
Condition()	A function that returns a new condition variable object. A condition variable allows one or more threads to wait until they are notified by another thread.
current_thread()	Returns the current Thread object, corresponding to the caller's thread of control. If the caller's thread of control was not created through the threading module, a dummy thread object with limited functionality is returned.
enumerate()	Returns a list of all Thread objects currently alive. The list includes daemonic threads, dummy thread objects created by current_thread(), and the main thread. It excludes terminated threads and threads that have not yet been started.
Event()	A function that returns a new event object. An event manages a flag that can be set to true with the set() method and reset to false with the clear() method. The wait() method blocks until the flag is true.
Lock()	A function that returns a new primitive lock object. Once a thread has acquired it, subsequent attempts to acquire it block, until it is released; any thread may release it.
RLock()	A function that returns a new re-entrant lock object. A re-entrant lock must be released by the thread that acquired it. Once a thread has acquired a re-entrant lock, the same thread may acquire it again without blocking; the thread must release it once for each time it has acquired it.
run()	The run() method is the entry point for a thread.
start()	The start() method starts a thread by calling the run() method.
join([time])	The join() waits for threads to terminate.
isAlive()	The isAlive() method checks whether a thread is still executing.
getName()	The getName() method returns the name of a thread.
setName()	The setName() method sets the name of a thread.

9.4 Creating Threads With Functions

Creating thread using functions takes the form

```
def fname():  # define a function
    statements

t = threading.Thread(target=fname, arg=[])  # create a thread object
t.start()  # start the thread
```

where t is a Thread object, target points to the function to call (fname), and arg lists the arguments to pass to the function.

Here is an example that illustrates thread creation from a function.

Program 9.1 creates two threads using the function worker(). The start() method starts the threads. The argument target=worker tells the thread to call worker() which in this case prints its name .

Program 9.1
```
import threading

def worker():
    print ('Worker')
    return

for i in range(2):
    t = threading.Thread(target=worker)
    t.start()
```

Output
```
Worker
Worker
```

Program 9.2 shows how to pass arguments to a thread function using args=(i,). It passes i to num in the worker() function which then prints its name and value. The comma in args=(i,) tells that you can pass more than one argument.

Program 9.2
```
import threading

def worker(num):
    print ('Worker: ', num)
    return

for i in range(2):
    w = threading.Thread(target=worker, args=(i,))
    w.start()
```

Output
```
Worker:   0
Worker:   1
```

Program 9.3 uses the getname() method to get the thread name, which the function prints with the label '– starting'. The thread sleeps for 2 seconds, and then exits with the message '- exiting.' But before it exits, the service() thread starts, sleeps for 3 seconds, and then exits after the worker() thread had exited. The exact order of execution of the threads will depend on their start time, sleep time, and other factors. In this case, the worker() thread started first, and then slept for 2 seconds. But before it exited, the service() thread had started and exited later after the worker() had exited.

Program 9.3
```
import threading
import time

def worker():
    print (threading.currentThread().getName(), '- starting')
    time.sleep(2)
    print (threading.currentThread().getName(), '- exiting')

def service():
    print (threading.currentThread().getName(), '- starting')
    time.sleep(3)
    print (threading.currentThread().getName(), '- exiting')

s = threading.Thread(name='service', target=service)
w = threading.Thread(name='worker', target=worker)

w.start()
s.start()
```

```
worker - starting
service - starting
worker - exiting
service - exiting
```

Program 9.4 is similar to the above except for the sleep times. The worker () started early but ended later than service () because it slept longer. So the order of execution has changed.

Program 9.4
```
import threading
import time

def worker():
    print ()
    print (threading.currentThread().getName(), '- starting')
    time.sleep(5)
    print (threading.currentThread().getName(), '- exiting')

def service():
    print (threading.currentThread().getName(), '- starting')
    time.sleep(3)
    print (threading.currentThread().getName(), '- exiting')

s = threading.Thread(name='service', target=service)
w = threading.Thread(name='worker', target=worker)

w.start()
s.start()
```

Output
```
worker - starting
service - starting
service - exiting
worker - exiting
```

Logging Module

Using the print function to debug/test threads is quite cumbersome. Fortunately, you can import the logging module to help you debug your code. You can import this module use the statement

```
import logging
```

The module takes the form

```
logging.basicConfig(level=logging.DEBUG, \
    format='[%(levelname)s] (%(threadName)s) %(message)s',)
```

What this module does is that it embeds the thread name in every log message using the formatter %(threadName)s. Including thread names in log messages makes debugging easier. The (threadName) and (message) are type casters - they convert string s to threadName and message types.

Program 9.5 illustrates how to use the logging module.

Program 9.5
```
import logging
import threading
import time
```

```
logging.basicConfig(level=logging.DEBUG, \
    format='[%(levelname)s] (%(threadName)s) %(message)s',)

def worker():
    logging.debug('- starting')
    time.sleep(2)
    logging.debug('- exiting')

def service():
    logging.debug('- starting')
    time.sleep(3)
    logging.debug('- exiting')

w = threading.Thread(name='worker', target=worker)
s = threading.Thread(name='service', target=service)

w.start()
s.start()
```

Output
```
[DEBUG] (worker    ) - starting
[DEBUG] (service   ) - starting
[DEBUG] (worker    ) - exiting
[DEBUG] (service   ) - exiting
```

Program 9.6 illustrates two thread functions: evenThread to generate even random numbers and oddThread to generate odd numbers, both in the range [1, 50]. It creates two threads - et and ot - using threading.Thread(target=evenThread, args=[]), and then starts the threads using the start() method. It prints one even number and one odd number.

Program 9.6
```
import threading
import random

def evenThread():
    x = random.randint(1,50)    # generates random number between 1 and 50
    if x % 2 == 0:              # testing for even number
        print (x)
    else:
        print (x+1)

def oddThread():
    x = random.randint(1,50)
    if x % 2 == 1:              # testing for odd number
        print (x)
    else:
        print (x+1)

et = threading.Thread(target=evenThread, args=[])
ot = threading.Thread(target=oddThread, args=[])
et.start()
ot.start()
```

Sample output
```
26
11
```

Program 9.7 is similar to the above but includes an argument to specify the number of random numbers to generate when the function is called. The evenThread generates 3 random numbers and the oddThread generates 4 random numbers.

Program 9.7
```
import threading
import random
def evenThread(n):
    print ('generating', n, 'even random numbers in [1,50]')
    for i in range (n):
        x = random.randint(1,50)
        if x % 2 == 0:
            print (x)
        else:
            print (x+1)

def oddThread(n):
    print ('generating', n, 'odd random numbers in [1,50]')
    for i in range (n):
        x = random.randint(1,50)
        if x % 2 == 1:
            print (x)
        else:
            print (x+1)

et = threading.Thread(target=evenThread, args=[3])
ot = threading.Thread(target=oddThread, args=[4])
et.start()
ot.start()
```

Output
```
generating 3 even random numbers in [1,50]
22
32
4
generating 4 odd random numbers in [1,50]
25
39
43
41
```

Program 9.8 sort of alternates the execution of these threads using the sleep() function. The evenThread generates 3 even random numbers, and then sleeps for 1 second; the oddThread generates 4 even random numbers, and then sleeps for 1 second. The process is repeated with another set of random numbers. The join() method ensures that the threads complete before terminating.

Program 9.8
```
import threading
import random
from time import sleep

def evenThread(n):
    nt = 2
    while nt > 0:
        print ('Generating', n, 'even random numbers in [1,50]')
        for i in range (n):
            x = random.randint(1,50)
            if x % 2 == 0:
                print (x)
            else:
                print (x+1)
        nt = nt - 1
        sleep(1)

def oddThread(n):
    nt = 2
```

152

```
    while nt > 0:
        print ('Generating', n, 'odd random numbers in [1,50]')
        for i in range (n):
            x = random.randint(1,50)
            if x % 2 == 1:
                print (x)
            else:
                print (x+1)
        nt = nt - 1
        sleep(1)
et = threading.Thread(target=evenThread, args=[3])
et.start()
ot = threading.Thread(target=oddThread, args=[4])
ot.start()

et.join()
ot.join()
```

Output
```
Generating 3 even random numbers in [1,50]
32
8
38
Generating 4 odd random numbers in [1,50]
21
23
27
37
Generating 3 even random numbers in [1,50]
34
48
34
Generating 4 odd random numbers in [1,50]
17
9
29
25
```

Program 9.9 passes two arguments to the function: name and number.

Program 9.9
```
from threading import Thread
from time import sleep

def func(name, n):
    for i in range(1, n):
        print(name,'i--->',i)
        sleep(1)

def test():
    t1 = Thread(target = func, args = ('Even-thread', 3))
    t2 = Thread(target = func, args = ('Odd-thread', 5))
    t1.start()
    t2.start()
    t1.join()
    t2.join()
    print ('Threads finished...exiting.')

test()
```

153

Output
```
Even-thread i---> 1
Odd-thread i---> 1
Even-thread i---> 2
Odd-thread i---> 2
Odd-thread i---> 3
Odd-thread i---> 4
Threads finished...exiting.
```

9.5 Creating Threads With Classes

The previous section discussed creating threads using functions. This section discusses creating threads using classes.

First, you define a child/subclass from the Thread class, and then override the base class constructor and run() methods. The start() method will automatically call the run() method.

Program 9.10 illustrates thread creation using classes. The sleep() function causes the thread to sleep for a random duration of between 1 and 5 seconds. This is to avoid executing the code so fast that we cannot keep follow the output. The join() method ensures that the threads complete before terminating.

Program 9.10
```python
from threading import Thread
from random import randint
import time

class MyThread(Thread):  # a child thread

    def __init__(self, val):  # constructor
        Thread.__init__(self)
        self.val = val

    def run(self):
        for i in range(1, self.val):
            print('Value %d in %s' % (i, self.getName()))
            sleep_time = randint(1, 5)
            print('%s sleeping for %d seconds...' % \
                    (self.getName(), sleep_time))
            time.sleep(sleep_time)

# main
if __name__ == '__main__':  # if the thread is main
    t1 = MyThread(2)
    t1.setName('Thread-1')

    t2 = MyThread(3)
    t2.setName('Thread-2')

    t1.start()
    t2.start()

    t1.join()
    t2.join()
    print('Main terminating...')
```

Sample output
```
Value 1 in Thread-1
Thread-1 sleeping for 2 seconds...
Value 1 in Thread-2
Thread-2 sleeping for 5 seconds...
```

```
Value 2 in Thread-2
Thread-2 sleeping for 5 seconds...
Main terminating...
```

Program 9.11 illustrates overriding parent class methods. It creates the MyThread subclass from Thread, then overrides the run() method. It creates 5 threads, and starts each one which calls the run() method.

Program 9.11
```
import threading
import logging

class MyThread(threading.Thread):

    def run(self):
        logging.debug('running')

logging.basicConfig(level=logging.DEBUG,
                    format='(%(threadName)-10s) %(message)s',)

for i in range(5):
    t = MyThread()
    t.start()
```

```
(Thread-61 ) running
(Thread-60 ) running
(Thread-64 ) running
(Thread-63 ) running
(Thread-62 ) running
```

Program 9.12 checks if a thread is alive using the is-alive() method.

Program 9.12
```
import threading
import time

class MyThread(threading.Thread):

    def run(self):
        time.sleep(5)

if __name__ == '__main__':
    for i in range(3):
        t = MyThread()
        t.start()
        print ('t is alive?', t.is_alive())
        t.join()
        print ('t is alive?', t.is_alive())
```

Sample output
```
t is alive? True
t is alive? False
t is alive? True
t is alive? False
t is alive? True
t is alive? False
```

Program 9.13 creates 5 threads and prints their ids.

Program 9.13
```
import threading

class MyThread (threading.Thread):

    def __init__(self, x):
        self.x = x
        threading.Thread.__init__(self)

    def run (self):
        print (str(self.x))

# Start 10 threads.
for x in range(5):
    t = MyThread(x)
    t.start()
```

```
0
1
2
3
4
```

Program 9.14 illustrate the `getname()` and `sleep()` methods.

Program 9.14
```
import threading
import time
import logging

def delayed():
    logging.debug('worker running')

logging.basicConfig(
    level=logging.DEBUG, format='(%(threadName)s) %(message)s',)

t1 = threading.Timer(0.3, delayed)
t1.setName('t1')
t2 = threading.Timer(0.3, delayed)
t2.setName('t2')

logging.debug('starting timers')
t1.start()
t2.start()

logging.debug('waiting before canceling %s', t2.getName())
time.sleep(0.2)
logging.debug('canceling %s', t2.getName())
t2.cancel()
logging.debug('done')
```

```
(MainThread) starting timers
(MainThread) waiting before canceling t2
(MainThread) canceling t2
(MainThread) done
(t1        ) worker running
```

9.6 Synchronizing Threads

Some applications require synchronizing threads - that is, allow them to communicate with each other. Event objects are used for this purpose. An Event manages an internal flag that callers can control with set() and clear() methods. Other threads can use the wait() method to pause until the flag is set, thus effectively blocking the progress until allowed to continue.

Program 9.15 illustrates synchronization of two threads - wait_event_timeout() and wait_event. The wait_event() *blocks* on a call to wait(), and does not return until the status of the event changes. The wait_event_timeout() checks the event status *without* blocking it.

The wait() method in the wait_event blocks the event whereas in the wait_event_timeout indicates the number of seconds the event will wait before timing out. It returns a Boolean value indicating whether or not the event is set, so the caller knows why the wait() returned. The is_set() method is used on the event without blocking.

Program 9.15

```
import logging
import threading
import time

# block event
def wait_event(e):
    logging.debug('wait_event starting')
    set_event = e.wait()
    logging.debug('event set: %s', set_event)

# non-block event
def wait_event_timeout(e, t):
    while not e.is_set():
        logging.debug('wait_event_timeout starting')
        set_event = e.wait(t)
        logging.debug('event set: %s', set_event)
        if set_event:
            logging.debug('processing event')
        else:
            logging.debug('doing other work')

logging.basicConfig(
    level=logging.DEBUG, format='(%(threadName)10s) %(message)s',)

e = threading.Event()
t1 = threading.Thread(name='block', target=wait_event, args=(e,),)
t1.start()

t2 = threading.Thread(name='nonblock', target=wait_event_timeout, args=(e,2),)
t2.start()

logging.debug('Waiting before calling Event.set()')
time.sleep(0.5)
e.set()
```

Output

```
(block    ) wait_event starting
(nonblock ) wait_event_timeout starting
(MainThread) Waiting before calling Event.set()
(MainThread) Event is set
(block    ) event set: True
(nonblock ) event set: True
(nonblock ) processing event
```

Program 9.16 also shows thread synchronization using the Lock object and the acquire() and release() methods on the Lock.

Program 9.16
```
import threading
import time

class myThread (threading.Thread):

    def __init__(self, id, name, counter):
        threading.Thread.__init__(self)
        self.id = id
        self.name = name
        self.counter = counter

    def run(self):
        print ('Starting ' + self.name)
        # acquire lock to synchronize threads
        tlock.acquire()
        print_time(self.name, self.counter, 3)
        # release ock to another thread
        tlock.release()

def print_time(name, delay, counter):
    while counter:
        time.sleep(delay)
        print ('%s: %s' % (name, time.ctime(time.time())))
        counter -= 1

tlock = threading.Lock()
threads = []

# create threads
t1 = myThread(1, 'Thread-1', 1)
t2 = myThread(2, 'Thread-2', 2)

# start threads
t1.start()
t2.start()

# appen threads to thread list
threads.append(t1)
threads.append(t2)

# wait for all threads to complete
for t in threads:
    t.join()
print ('\nExiting Main Thread')
```

Output
```
Starting Thread-1
Starting Thread-2
Thread-1: Tue Feb 13 12:00:42 2018
Thread-1: Tue Feb 13 12:00:43 2018
Thread-1: Tue Feb 13 12:00:44 2018
Thread-2: Tue Feb 13 12:00:46 2018
Thread-2: Tue Feb 13 12:00:48 2018
Thread-2: Tue Feb 13 12:00:50 2018
Exiting Main Thread
```

9.7 Accessing Shared Resources

In some applications, mutual exclusion to shared resources is crucial and required. This is similar to processing transactions in a database where only one process should be given access to update a record at any given time. This also applies to threads sharing resources. Only one thread should be given access to update a shared resource at any given time. Allowing multiple threads to update shared resources simultaneously could lead to errors which are hard to detect.

The threading module provides the Lock mechanism to control/restrict access to shared resources. Access to shared resources is implemented as follows:

1. Create a Lock object for the shared resource.
2. Acquire the lock by calling the acquire() method. If the lock is not available, the thread must wait until it can acquire it.
3. Update the shared resource.
4. Release the lock by calling the release() method.

Once a thread releases the lock, other threads can acquire the lock and update the resource.

The code for updating a shared resource take the form

```
lock = Lock()
lock.acquire() # will block the thread if the lock is not available
... access shared resources
lock.release()
```

Normally, you will use the **try-finally** statement when acquiring a lock. But you can also use the **with** statement. The with automatically acquires the lock before entering the code block, and releases it when leaving the block. The code for this is as follows:

```
with lock:
... access the shared resource
```

The acquire() method takes an optional wait flag, which is used to avoid blocking if the lock is held by another thread. If you pass False, the method never blocks, but will return False if the lock is held by another thread. The code for this is as follows:

```
if not lock.acquire(False):
    ... failed to lock the resource
else:
    try:
        ... access shared resource
    finally:
        lock.release()
```

You can use the locked() method to check if the lock is held by another thread. You cannot use this method to check if a call to acquire would block the thread or not; some other thread may have acquired the lock between the method call and the next statement. The code for this is as follows:

```
if not lock.locked():
    # some other thread may run before we get
    # to the next line
    lock.acquire() # may block anyway
```

Using Locks to Synchronize Threads

Locks can also be used to synchronize threads. The methods used for implementing this are Event (), wait (), set (), clear () and condition ().

An event is a simple synchronization object; it represents an internal flag, and threads can wait for the flag to be set, or set or clear the flag themselves. The code for this is as follows:

```
event = threading.Event()

# wait for the flag to be set
event.wait()

# set or reset or clear it
event.set()
event.clear()
```

If the flag is set, the **wait ()** method does nothing. If the flag is clear, **wait** will block until it becomes set again. Any number of threads may wait for the same event.

A condition is an advanced version of the event object. It represents some kind of state change in the application, and a thread can wait for a given condition, or signal that the condition has occurred. The code for this is as follows:

```
# create a condition object
condition = threading.Condition()
```

Here is a simple consumer/producer example. The producer thread needs to acquire the condition object before it can notify the consumer threads that a new item is now available as in the code below.

```
# producer thread
... produce an item

condition.acquire()
... add the item to resource
condition.notify() # signal that a new item is available
condition.release()
```

The consumer thread must acquire the condition (and the related lock), and then can attempt to fetch the item from the resource as in the code below.

```
# consumer thread
condition.acquire()

while True:
    ... get item from resource
    if item:
        break
    condition.wait() # sleep until item becomes available

condition.release()
... process item
```

The wait () method releases the lock, blocks the current thread until another thread calls the notify () or notifyAll () method on the same condition, then re-acquires the lock. If multiple threads are waiting, the **notify** method wakes up one of the threads, while the **notifyAll** method will wake up all the threads.

To avoid blocking in **wait**, you can pass in a timeout value (a floating-point value). If given, the method will return after the given timeout, even if the **notify()** method hasn't been called. If you use a timeout, you must inspect the resource to see if something actually happened.

9.8 Daemon vs. Non-Daemon Threads

This far, our programs have implicitly waited to exit until all threads had completed their work. Programs can also spawn *daemon* threads that run *without* blocking the main program.

Daemon threads are useful in certain situations such as when a thread should not be interrupted in the midst of doing some critical computation. To make a daemon thread, you use the setDaemon() method with the argument True. The default setting for threads is non-daemon.

Program 9.17 illustrates daemon threads. The output for the daemon thread does not include the – exiting message. This is because all non-daemon threads (including the main thread) will exit before the daemon thread wakes up from its sleep.

Program 9.17
```
import threading
import time
import logging

logging.basicConfig(level=logging.DEBUG, \
        format='(%(threadName)-10s) %(message)s',)

def daemon():
    logging.debug('- starting')
    time.sleep(3)
    logging.debug('- exiting')

def ndaemon():
    logging.debug('- starting')
    logging.debug('- exiting')

td = threading.Thread(name='daemon', target=daemon)
td.setDaemon(True)

tn = threading.Thread(name='non-daemon', target=ndaemon)

td.start()
tn.start()
```

Output
```
[DEBUG] (daemon    ) - starting
[DEBUG] (non-daemon) - starting
[DEBUG] (non-daemon) - exiting
[DEBUG] (daemon    ) - exiting
```

You can also call the join() method to wait until a daemon thread has completed its work.

Program 9.18 illustrates this. Waiting for the daemon thread to exit on join() means it might display the message – exiting. Note that the daeman thread always exits last.

Program 9.18
```
import threading
import time
import logging

logging.basicConfig(level=logging.DEBUG, \
    format='(%(threadName)-10s) %(message)s',)

def daemon():
    logging.debug('- starting')
    time.sleep(2)
    logging.debug('- exiting')

def ndaemon():
    logging.debug('- starting')
    logging.debug('- exiting')

td = threading.Thread(name='daemon', target=daemon)
td.setDaemon(True)

tn = threading.Thread(name='non-daemon', target=ndaemon)

td.start()
tn.start()

td.join()
tn.join()
```

Output
```
[DEBUG] (daemon    ) - starting
[DEBUG] (non-daemon) - starting
[DEBUG] (non-daemon) - exiting
[DEBUG] (daemon    ) - exiting
```

The join() method blocks the thread indefinitely. However, you can pass a timeout argument to wait for the thread to become inactive. If the thread does not complete within this time, the join() method returns. In this case, as the the timeout passed is less than the amount of time the daemon thread slept, the thread is still alive after the join() method returns.

Program 9.19 illustrates this.

Program 9.19
```
import threading
import time
import logging

logging.basicConfig(level=logging.DEBUG, \
    format='(%(threadName)-10s) %(message)s',)

def daemon():
    logging.debug('- starting')
    time.sleep(2)
    logging.debug('- exiting')

def ndaemon():
    logging.debug('- starting')
    logging.debug('- exiting')

td = threading.Thread(name='daemon', target=daemon)
td.setDaemon(True)
```

162

```
tn = threading.Thread(name='non-daemon', target=ndaemon)

td.start()
tn.start()

td.join(1)
print ('td.isAlive()', td.isAlive())
tn.join()
```

Output
```
[DEBUG] (daemon    ) - starting
[DEBUG] (non-daemon) - starting
[DEBUG] (non-daemon) - exiting
td.isAlive() True
[DEBUG] (daemon    ) - exiting
```

9.9 Enumerating Threads

The enumerate() method is useful for listing all active Thread instances.

Program 9.20 illustrates this. As the worker sleeps for a random amount of time, the output would vary.

Program 9.20
```
import random
import threading
import time
import logging

logging.basicConfig(level=logging.DEBUG, \
    format='(%(threadName)-10s) %(message)s',)

def worker():
    pause = random.randint(1, 5)
    logging.debug('sleeping %s', pause)
    time.sleep(pause)
    logging.debug('ending')
    return

for i in range(3):
    t = threading.Thread(target=worker)
    t.setDaemon(True)
    t.start()

main_thread = threading.currentThread()
t = threading.currentThread()
for t in threading.enumerate():
    if t is main_thread:
        continue
    logging.debug('joining %s', t.getName())
    t.join()
```

Output
```
(Thread-7  ) sleeping 5
(MainThread) joining Thread-4
(Thread-8  ) sleeping 2
(Thread-8  ) ending
(Thread-6  ) ending
(Thread-7  ) ending
```

Program 9.21 has two threads – Even and Odd. Even generates 3 even random numbers between 1 and 49, then sleeps, and finally exits. Odd generates 5 odd random numbers between 50 and 99, then sleeps, and finally exits. The order of execution of the threads will depend on the sleep time and other factors. The code shows output for two sample runs.

Program 9.21

```
import threading
import random
import time

def even(n):
    print (threading.currentThread().getName(), '- starting')
    print ('I am generating %s even numbers between 1 and 49:' %n)
    for i in range (n):
        r = random.randint(1, 49)
        if r%2 == 0:
            print (r)
        else:
            print (r+1)
    time.sleep(3)
    print (threading.currentThread().getName(), '- exiting')

def odd(n):
    print (threading.currentThread().getName(), '- starting')
    print ('I am generating %s odd numbers between 50 and 99:' %n)
    for i in range (n):
        r = random.randint(50, 100)
        if r%2 == 1:
            print (r)
        else:
            print (r+1)
    time.sleep(3)
    print (threading.currentThread().getName(), '- exiting')

te = threading.Thread(name = 'Even thread', target=even, args=(3,))
to = threading.Thread(name = 'Odd thread', target=odd, args=(5,))

te.start()
time.sleep(5)
to.start()
```

Sample Output 1

```
Even thread - starting
I am generating 3 even numbers between 1 and 49:
18
20
14
Odd thread - starting
I am generating 5 odd numbers between 50 and 99:
69
63
83
75
55
Even thread - exiting
Odd thread - exiting
```

Sample Output 2

```
Even thread - starting
I am generating 3 even numbers between 1 and 49:
14
18
```

164

```
36
Even thread - exiting
Odd thread - starting
I am generating 5 odd numbers between 50 and 99:
99
89
83
65
71
Odd thread - exiting
```

9.10 Sample Programs

This section gives more thread examples.

Program 9.22 creates two threads – t1 and t2 – from the myThread class. Then it starts the threads by calling the start() method which in turn calls the run() method. The run() method starts the print_time() function, then sleeps for 3 seconds for each thread. The join() method ensures that the threads complete before terminating.

Program 9.22
```python
import threading
import time

class myThread (threading.Thread):

    def __init__(self, id, name, counter):
        threading.Thread.__init__(self)
        self.id = id
        self.name = name
        self.counter = counter

    def run(self):
        print ('Starting ' + self.name)
        print_time(self.name, self.counter, 3)
        print ('Exiting ' + self.name)

def print_time(name, delay, counter):
    while counter:
        time.sleep(delay)
        print ('%s: %s' % (name, time.ctime(time.time())))
        counter -= 1

# Create new threads
t1 = myThread(1, 'Thread-1', 1)
t2 = myThread(2, 'Thread-2', 2)

# Start new Threads
t1.start()
t2.start()
t1.join()
t2.join()
print ('Exiting Main thread')
```

Sample output
```
Starting Thread-1
Starting Thread-2
Thread-1: Tue Feb 13 14:24:20 2018
Thread-1: Tue Feb 13 14:24:21 2018
Thread-2: Tue Feb 13 14:24:21 2018
```

165

```
Thread-1: Tue Feb 13 14:24:22 2018
Exiting Thread-1
Thread-2: Tue Feb 13 14:24:23 2018
Thread-2: Tue Feb 13 14:24:25 2018
Exiting Thread-2
Exiting Main thread
```

Program 9.23 creates two threads – t1 and t2 – and starts the threads which in turn calls the run() method. Each thread sleeps for a duration of between 1 and 5 seconds.

Program 9.23
```
from threading import Thread
from random import randint
import time

class MyThread(Thread):

    def __init__(self, val):        # constructor
        Thread.__init__(self)
        self.val = val

    def run(self):
        for i in range(1, self.val):
            sleeptime = randint(1, 5)
            print('%s sleeping for %d seconds...' % \
                    (self.getName(), sleeptime))
            time.sleep(sleeptime)   # sleep

t1 = MyThread(3)                # create a thread object
t1.setName('Thread-1')          # set its name

t2 = MyThread(3)
t2.setName('Thread-2')

# run the threads
t1.start()
t2.start()

# wait for threads to finish...
t1.join()
t2.join()

print('main terminating...')
```

Sample output
```
Thread-1
Thread-1 sleeping for 1 seconds...
Thread-2
Thread-2 sleeping for 4 seconds...
Thread-1
Thread-1 sleeping for 1 seconds...
Thread-2
Thread-2 sleeping for 1 seconds...
main terminating...
```

Program 9.24 illustrates threading with the class Queue (imported from queue module) and its methods get() and put(). It creates the queue q, then puts an integer random number (between 1 and 50) into it using the put() method and later gets an item from q using the get() method.

166

Program 9.24
```
from threading import Thread
from random import randint
import queue
import time

def thread1(name, q):
    #read variable "a" modify by thread 2
    while True:
        item = q.get()
        if item is None:
            return
        print (item)

def thread2(name, q):
    for i in range(5):
        q.put(randint(1, 50))
        time.sleep(1)
    q.put(None) # Poison pill

q = queue.Queue()
t1 = Thread(target=thread1, args=("Thread-1", q) )
t2 = Thread(target=thread2, args=("Thread-2", q) )

t1.start()
t2.start()
t1.join()
t2.join()
```

Sample Output
```
33
48
10
32
39
```

Exercise

1. What are threads? Give a scenario where threads could be applied.

2. Create and run a thread using function; make the thread to sleep for 3 seconds before terminating.

3. Create and run two threads - Thread-1, Thread-2 – using function; make the thread to sleep for a random amount time between 1 to 5 seconds.

4. Do question (3) by passing the thread name and argument for sleep time.

5. Create and start and run two threads as follows:

6. Prime to generate 3 prime numbers.

7. Odd to generate 5 integer random number between 1 and 20.

8. Do question (5) such that the process is repeated 2 times (Prime...Odd...Prime...Odd)

9. Do question (2) using class.

10. Do question (3) using class.

11. Do question (4) using class.

12. Do question (5) using class.

13. Create two threads such that only one thread is allowed to update a variable at any given time.

14. Create two threads – producer and consumer – such that the producer produces an item and the consumer consumes the item; do that for 5 items.

15. What are daeman threads?

16. Create two threads – sender and receiver – such that the sender sends hello to the receiver and waits until it receives an acknowledgment from the receiver.

## Chapter 10

Database

Learning Outcomes:

After completing this chapter, the student will be able to

- *Explain what a database is.*
- *Create databases.*
- *Use SQL commands to insert, delete, update and fetch records.*
- *Use aggregate functions.*
- *Work with multiple tables*

10.1 What is a Database?

A (relational) database is an organized collection of data. The data are typically organized to model real-life entities such as people, things, places, events and concepts. The term *database* is often used to refer to both data in a database as well as the database software (e.g., SQLite, SQL Server, My SQL, Access and Oracle). The database software allows users and other software to interact with the database.

This chapter will use SQLite to illustrate the various database operations. But it will equally apply to other databases as well.

Python uses the database interface DB-API. This provides a common interface, which can be used to access all relational databases.

10.2 Database Concepts

A database is a collection of *related* tables for an application. The tables are related (linked) through foreign keys.

A table is a collection of rows and columns. The columns correspond to fields (attributes) and the rows correspond to records (tuples). The rows need not be named. The columns however must be named.

All columns in a table must have *unique* names, meaning, no two columns can have the same name. Similarly, the rows in the table must be unique. The unique *key* value makes each row unique.

The order of columns and rows in a table is not significant. That means, you can exchange rows and columns and these will not have any effect on the database.

A table typically has a *primary key* consisting of a single or a combination of fields (columns). Each key value is unique and this guarantees uniqueness of the records (rows).

The database software uses the key to create an index table that is used for sorting and searching. This improves the speed of database operations.

In addition to the the primary key, a table may also have *foreign keys*. The foreign key in a table is used to access another table in the database where it is the primary key. For example, a `product` table may have a column for `supplier_code` where it is the *primary key* in the `supplier` table.

10.3 SQL Commands

SQL is the language that you use to work with databases. There are several SQL commands in the language, the basic ones being:

SQL Command	Description
CREATE TABLE	Create a database table
INSERT INTO	Insert records into a database
DELETE FROM	Delete records from a database
DROP TABLE	Drop table from a database
UPDATE...SET	Update records in a database
SELECT FROM WHERE	Query a database

Let's discuss each of these commands very briefly.

CREATE TABLE

This command takes the form:

```
CREATE TABLE product (
prod_id INTEGER PRIMARY KEY,
prod_name VARCHAR(20),
quantity INTEGER,
price DECIMAL (7, 2));
```

It creates the table `product` with fields `prod_id`, `prod_name`, `quantity` and `price` (in 7 columns with 2 decimal places). The SQLite data types INTEGER, VARCHAR and DECIMAL correspond to the Python data types `int`, `str` and `float`. The command also specifies `prod_id` as the primary key.

INSERT INTO VALUES

This command takes the form:

```
INSERT INTO product (field names) VALUES (field values)
```

Here is an example.

```
INSERT INTO product (prod_id, prod_name, quantity, price)
                    VALUES (1, 'iPhone10', 5, 1499.90);
```

It assigns values to the various `product` fields.

UPDATE SET WHERE

This command takes the form:

```
UPDATE product
SET price = 1500
WHERE (prod_id = 1);
```

Set the product price to 1500 for `prod_id = 1`

DELETE FROM

This command takes the form:

```
DELETE FROM product WHERE (prod_id = 1);
```

This deletes the record for prod_id = 1.

DROP TABLE

This command takes the form:

```
DROP TABLE product
```

This drops the product table from the database.

SELECT FROM WHERE

This command takes the form:

```
SELECT prod_id, prod_name, price
FROM product
WHERE (price > 1000);
```

This will select all records with price > 1000.

Another version of the command is

```
SELECT *
FROM product
WHERE (price > 1000);
```

The * will select all fields. If we drop the WHERE clause, it will select all records.

The table below gives a list of commonly used methods/attributes for working with databases.

Method/Attribute	Description
cursor()	Accepts a single optional parameter factory.
commit()	Saves (commits) the current transaction. If you don't call this method, you would lose the transaction information.
close()	Closes the database connection. Note that this does not automatically call commit(). If you close the connection without calling commit() first, changes will be lost!
connection	Provides the SQLite database Connection used by the Cursor object. A Cursor object created by calling con.cursor() will have a connection attribute that refers to con:
execute(sql [, parameters])	Creates an intermediate cursor object by calling the cursor method, then calls the cursor's execute method with the parameters given.
executemany(sql [, parameters])	Creates an intermediate cursor object by calling the cursor method, then calls the cursor's executemany method with the parameters given.
executescript(sql_ script)	Creates an intermediate cursor object by calling the cursor method, then calls the cursor's executescript method with the parameters given.
fetchone()	Fetches the next row of a query result set, returning a single sequence, or None when no more data is available.
fetchmany()	Fetches the next set of rows of a query result, returning a list. An empty list is returned when no more rows are available.

`fetchall()`	Fetches all (remaining) rows of a query result, returning a list. Note that the cursor's arraysize attribute can affect the performance of this operation. An empty list is returned when no rows are available.
`rollback()`	Rolls back any changes to the database since the last call to commit().
`rowcount`	Number of rows affected/selected.

10.4 Creating Database

Let's say we want to create the below database product with table product. (It's OK to have the same name for both the database and table as their different file extensions make them unique.).

product

prod_id	prod_name	quantity	price
1	iPhone10	5	1200.75
2	iPad7	7	1500.55
3	Laptop	2	2900.95

To create the product database table using SQLite3, you can use the following steps:

1) Create a `connection` object for the database.

2) Create a `cursor` object using the connection in (1).

3) Create the product table using the SQL command `CREATE TABLE`.

4) Execute the SQL command in (3) using the `execute` method.

5) Insert records into the product table using the SQL command `INSERT INTO`.

6) Execute the SQL command in (5) with the `execute` method.

7) Repeat steps (5) and (6) for additional records.

8) Save the records using the `commit` method.

9) Close the database connection using the `close` method.

Program 10.1 illustrates these steps.

• The import `sqlite3` imports the `sqlite3` module into the program.

• The statement

```
connection = sqlite3.connect('product.db')
```

creates a `connection` string for the `product` database.

• The statement

```
cursor = connection.cursor()
```

creates a `cursor` object that keeps track of the records fetched from a database query.

- The statement

```
sql_command = """
CREATE TABLE product (
prod_id INTEGER PRIMARY KEY,
prod_name VARCHAR(20),
qty INTEGER,
price DECIMAL (7, 2)); """
```

declares the `product` table.

The variable `sql_command` stores the SQL command. (The command spans several lines but it doesn't require the statement breaker character \.) The command is enclosed between a pair of triple quotes `"""` (you can also use single triple quotes `'''`).

The command specifies the various table fields: `prod_id`, `prod_name`, `qty` and `price` - and their data types `INTEGER`, `VARCHAR` and `DECIMAL(7,2)`. These database data types correspond to Python's data type int, string and float (with 2 decimal places) respectively. It also declares the `prod_id` as the `PRIMARY KEY` (a unique field used for sorting and searching records in the table).

The (first) `cursor.execute(sql_command)` executes the above SQL command. (Note the object notation: `cursor` is the object; `execute` is its method; and `sql_command` is its argument/parameter.

The program does not produce any output as it only defines and saves database structure.

Program 10.1

```
# create database structure

import sqlite3

# connection string
connection = sqlite3.connect('product.db')
cursor = connection.cursor()

# sql command to create the product table
sql_command = """
CREATE TABLE product (
prod_id INTEGER PRIMARY KEY,
prod_name VARCHAR(20),
qty INTEGER,
price DECIMAL (7, 2)); """

# execute the sql command to create the table
cursor.execute(sql_command)

# close the connection
connection.close()
```

10.5 Inserting Records into Database

The previous section defined the database structure, but the database is empty – it has no records. This section shows how to populate the database using the SQL command INSERT INTO.

Program 10.2 inserts 3 records into the database.

- The statement

```
sql_command = """INSERT INTO product (prod_id, prod_name, qty, price)VALUES
(NULL, 'iPhone10', 5, 1200.75); """
```

inserts a record into the table. It specifies the fields and their respective values (strings must be enclosed in quotes).

- The (second) cursor.execute(sql_command) executes the above INSERT command.

- The connection.commit() statement commits (saves) the records in the disk.

- The connection.close() statement closes the database connection.

The program does not produce any output as it populates the database (with three records).

Program 10.2

```
# populate database

import sqlite3

# connection string
connection = sqlite3.connect('product.db')
cursor = connection.cursor()

# sql command to create the product table
sql_command = """
CREATE TABLE product (
prod_id INTEGER PRIMARY KEY,
prod_name VARCHAR(20),
qty INTEGER,
price DECIMAL (7, 2)); """

# execute the sql command to create the table
cursor.execute(sql_command)

# insert a record into the product table
sql_command = """INSERT INTO product (prod_id, prod_name, qty, price)
    VALUES (NULL, 'iPhone10', 5, 1200.75); """
cursor.execute(sql_command)

# insert another record
sql_command = """INSERT INTO product (prod_id, prod_name, qty, price)
    VALUES (NULL, 'iPad7', 7, 1500.95); """
cursor.execute(sql_command)

sql_command = """INSERT INTO product (prod_id, prod_name, qty, price)
    VALUES (NULL, 'Desktop', 7, 2500.55); """
cursor.execute(sql_command)

# commit/save the records
connection.commit()
```

```
# close the connection
connection.close()
```

10.6 Fetching Records

In the previous section, we populated the database. This section shows how to retrieve (fetch) records in the database using the SQL command SELECT...FROM. This command allows you to fetch all the records or only some of the records based on a certain criteria.

Program 10.3 illustrates this. It fetches and displays *all* the records in the product table.

The SQL command

```
SELECT * FROM product
```

is used to fetch all records in the table. The asterisk * denotes all fields in the table.

The statement

```
cursor.execute("SELECT * FROM product")
```

executes the above SELECT command.

The statement

```
result = cursor.fetchall()
```

fetches *all* the records in product and stores them in result (a list). The cursor method for fetching all the records is fetchall().

The for statement then prints the records in result one by one.

The last group of statements is similar to the above but prints only *one* (the first) record using the method fetchone().

Program 10.3
```
import sqlite3
connection = sqlite3.connect("product.db")
cursor = connection.cursor()

cursor.execute("SELECT * FROM product")
print("List of records in product table:")
result = cursor.fetchall()
for rec in result:
    print(rec)

cursor.execute("SELECT * FROM product")
print("\nFirst record:")
res = cursor.fetchone()
print(res)

connection.close()
```

Output
```
List of records in product table:
(1, 'iPhone10', 5, 1200.75)
(2, 'iPad7', 7, 1500.95)
(3, 'Desktop', 7, 2500.55)
```

```
First record:
(1, 'iPhone10', 5, 1200.75)
```

Program 10.4 shows how to fetch records selectively – records meeting a certain criteria. It fetches records that meet the following criteria:

(1) price is greater than 1300,
(2) price is less than 2500 and
(3) prod_name is equal to iPad7.

Note how the criteria are specified in the SELECT commands including the BETWEEN...AND criteria.

Program 10.4

```python
import sqlite3

connection = sqlite3.connect("product.db")
cursor = connection.cursor()

cursor.execute("SELECT * FROM product WHERE price > 1300;")
print("Records with price > 1300:")
result = cursor.fetchall()
for rec in result:
    print(rec)

cursor.execute("SELECT * FROM product WHERE price < 2500;")
print("\nRecords with price < 2500:")
result = cursor.fetchall()
for rec in result:
    print(rec)

cursor.execute("SELECT * FROM product WHERE price BETWEEN \
                1200 AND 1300;")
print("\nRecords with price between 1200 and 1300:")
result = cursor.fetchall()
for rec in result:
    print(rec)

cursor.execute("SELECT * FROM product WHERE prod_name = 'iPad7';")
print("\niPad7 Records:")
result = cursor.fetchall()
for rec in result:
    print(rec)

connection.close()
```

Output
```
Records with price > 1300:
(2, 'iPad7', 7, 1500.95)
(3, 'Desktop', 7, 2500.55)

Records with price < 2500:
(1, 'iPhone10', 5, 1200.75)
(2, 'iPad7', 7, 1500.95)

Records with price between 1200 and 1300:
(1, 'iPhone10', 5, 1200.75)

iPad7 Records:
(2, 'iPad7', 7, 1500.95)
```

10.7 Displaying Records in Different Formats

The previous programs displayed the results in *list* form. If you want to display the results differently, you need to store the individual items in variables and then print them according to your preferred format as shown in Program 10.5.

Program 10.5
```
import sqlite3

connection = sqlite3.connect("product.db")
cursor = connection.cursor()

cursor.execute("SELECT * FROM product")
print("List of records in product table:")
result = cursor.fetchall() # result is a list

for rec in result:
    prod_id = rec[0]
    prod_name = rec[1]
    qty = rec[2]
    price = rec[3]
    print ("ProdID = %s, ProdName = %s, Quantity = %d, Price = %.2f" \
              %(prod_id, prod_name, qty, price))

connection.close()
```

```
List of records in product table:
ProdID = 1, ProdName = iPhone10, Quantity = 5, Price = 1200.75
ProdID = 2, ProdName = iPad7, Quantity = 7, Price = 1500.95
ProdID = 3, ProdName = Desktop, Quantity = 7, Price = 2500.55
```

10.8 Inserting Records from Lists

In Program 10.2, we populated the database with 3 records by entering the data directly into the INSERT command. Let's now add 3 more records - this time using data from a list - new_prod - as in Program 10.6. The list items (records) are tuples enclosed between (). The cursor method executemany () inserts into the database all the records in the list. The ? mark inside VALUES act as placeholders for the various record fields.

```
cursor.executemany(("""INSERT INTO product (prod_id, prod_name, \
             qty, price)VALUES (?, ?, ?, ?)""", new_prod))
```

Program 10.6
```
import sqlite3

connection = sqlite3.connect("product.db")
cursor = connection.cursor()

new_prod = [ (4, 'Dell Quantum', 2, 2550.00),
             (5, 'HP GPU', 7, 2900.90),
             (6, 'IBM ThinkPad', 3, 1980.00) ]

# add the above 3 new products
cursor.executemany("""INSERT INTO product (prod_id, prod_name, \
                  qty, price)VALUES (?, ?, ?, ?)""", new_prod)

cursor.execute("SELECT * FROM product")
```

```
print("List of records in product table:")
result = cursor.fetchall()

for rec in result:
    prod_id = rec[0]
    prod_name = rec[1]
    qty = rec[2]
    price = rec[3]
    print ("ProdID = %s, ProdName = %s, Quantity = %d, \
            Price = %.2f" % (prod_id, prod_name, qty, price))

connection.commit()
connection.close()
```

Output
```
List of records in product table:
ProdID = 1, ProdName = iPhone10, Quantity = 5, Price = 1200.75
ProdID = 2, ProdName = iPad7, Quantity = 7, Price = 1500.95
ProdID = 3, ProdName = Desktop, Quantity = 7, Price = 2500.55
ProdID = 4, ProdName = Dell Quantum, Quantity = 2, Price = 2550.00
ProdID = 5, ProdName = HP GPU, Quantity = 7, Price = 2900.90
ProdID = 6, ProdName = IBM ThinkPad, Quantity = 3, Price = 1980.00
```

10.9 Deleting Records

To delete records from a database, we use the SQL command DELETE FROM.

Program 10.7 illustrates this. It INSERTs a product with key value 66, and then deletes it. It prints the *before* and *after* version of the database.

Program10.7
```
import sqlite3

connection = sqlite3.connect("product.db")
cursor = connection.cursor()

cursor.execute("""INSERT INTO product (prod_id, prod_name, \
                qty, price) VALUES (66, 'Quantum Pro', 1, 20000);""")

cursor.execute("SELECT * FROM product")
print("List of records in product after insertion:")
result = cursor.fetchall()

for rec in result:
    print (rec)

cursor.execute('''DELETE FROM product WHERE prod_id = 66;''')
result = cursor.fetchall()

cursor.execute("SELECT * FROM product")
print("\nList of records in product after deletion:")
result = cursor.fetchall()

for rec in result:
    print (rec)

connection.commit()
connection.close()
```

Output
```
List of records in product after insertion:
```

```
(1, 'iPhone10', 5, 1200.75)
(2, 'iPad7', 7, 1500.95)
(3, 'Desktop', 7, 2500.55)
(4, 'Dell Quantum', 2, 2550)
(5, 'HP GPU', 7, 2900.9)
(6, 'IBM ThinkPad', 3, 1980)
(66, 'Quantum Pro', 1, 20000)

List of records in product after deletion:
(1, 'iPhone10', 5, 1200.75)
(2, 'iPad7', 7, 1500.95)
(3, 'Desktop', 7, 2500.55)
(4, 'Dell Quantum', 2, 2550)
(5, 'HP GPU', 7, 2900.9)
(6, 'IBM ThinkPad', 3, 1980)
```

Here is another example. Program 10.8 deletes all the records with `price > 2000`.

Program 10.8

```
import sqlite3

connection = sqlite3.connect("product.db")
cursor = connection.cursor()

cursor.execute("""INSERT INTO product (prod_id, prod_name, \
            qty, price) VALUES (66, 'Quantum Pro', 1, 20000);""")

cursor.execute("SELECT * FROM product")
print("List of records in product after insertion:")
result = cursor.fetchall()
for rec in result:
    print (rec)

cursor.execute('''DELETE FROM product WHERE price > 2000''')
result = cursor.fetchall()

cursor.execute("SELECT * FROM product")
print("\nList of records in product after deletion:")
result = cursor.fetchall()
for rec in result:
    print (rec)

connection.commit()
connection.close()
```

Output
```
List of records in product after insertion:
(1, 'iPhone10', 5, 1200.75)
(2, 'iPad7', 7, 1500.95)
(3, 'Desktop', 7, 2500.55)
(4, 'Dell Quantum', 2, 2550)
(5, 'HP GPU', 7, 2900.9)
(6, 'IBM ThinkPad', 3, 1980)
(66, 'Quantum Pro', 1, 20000)

List of records in product after deletion:
(1, 'iPhone10', 5, 1200.75)
(2, 'iPad7', 7, 1500.95)
(6, 'IBM ThinkPad', 3, 1980)
```

You can also drop an entire database table (i.e. all the records) by using the SQL command DROP TABLE.

Program 10.9 illustrates this. It drops the product table from the database.

Program 10.9
```
import sqlite3

connection = sqlite3.connect("product.db")
cursor = connection.cursor()

sql_command = '''DROP TABLE product;'''
cursor.execute(sql_command)

connection.commit()
connection.close()
```

10.10 Updating Records

To update records in a database, use the SQL command UPDATE...SET.

Program 10.10 illustrates this. It UPDATEs *all* the records by SETting their price to 1000.

Program 10.10
```
import sqlite3
connection = sqlite3.connect("product.db")
cursor = connection.cursor()

sql_command = """SELECT * FROM product; """
cursor.execute(sql_command)
result = cursor.fetchall()

for rec in result:
    print(rec)

cursor.execute("""UPDATE product SET price = 1000;""")

result = cursor.fetchall()

for rec in result:
    print(rec)

connection.commit()

connection.close()
```

Output
```
(1, 'iPhone10', 5, 1000)
(2, 'iPad7', 7, 1000)
(3, 'Desktop', 7, 1000)
(4, 'Dell Quantum', 2, 1000)
(5, 'HP GPU', 7, 1000)
(6, 'IBM ThinkPad', 3, 1000)
```

You can also update records *selectively* by specify a criteria. Program 10.11 illustrates this. It SETs the price of products to 2000, 3000 and 5000 for prod_id = 1, prod_id = 3 and prod_id = 5 respectively. It also shows the database records *before* and *after* the UPDATE operation.

Program 10.11
```
import sqlite3
connection = sqlite3.connect("product.db")
cursor = connection.cursor()

sql_command = """SELECT * FROM product; """
```

```
cursor.execute(sql_command)
result = cursor.fetchall()

for rec in result:
    print(rec)

cursor.execute("""UPDATE product SET price = 2000 \
            WHERE prod_id = 1;""")
cursor.execute("""UPDATE product SET price = 3000 \
            WHERE prod_id = 3;""")
cursor.execute("""UPDATE product SET price = 12000 \
            WHERE prod_id = 5;""")
connection.commit()

result = cursor.fetchall()

for rec in result:
    print(rec)

connection.close()
```

Output
```
(1, 'iPhone10', 5, 2000)
(2, 'iPad7', 7, 1000)
(3, 'Desktop', 7, 3000)
(4, 'Dell Quantum', 2, 1000)
(5, 'HP GPU', 7, 12000)
(6, 'IBM ThinkPad', 3, 1000)
```

Replacing

```
cursor.execute("""UPDATE product SET price = 2000 \
            WHERE prod_id = 1;""")
```

with

```
cursor.execute("""UPDATE product SET prod_name = 'iPhone12', \
            price = 2700 WHERE prod_id = 1;""")
```

in the above program will produce the following output:

```
(1, 'iPhone12', 5, 2700)
(2, 'iPad7', 7, 1000)
(3, 'Desktop', 7, 3000)
(4, 'Dell Quantum', 2, 1000)
(5, 'HP GPU', 7, 12000)
(6, 'IBM ThinkPad', 3, 1000)
```

10.11 Aggregate Functions

Aggregate functions perform computations on columns (fields), for example, the sum/total, average, minimum and maximum. You can use these functions to generate summary information.

Here is the list of aggregate functions:

Function	Description
avg(x)	Returns the average value of all non-NULL x within a group. The result is always a floating point value
count(*)	Returns the total number of rows in the group.
count(x)	Returns a count of the number of times that x is not NULL in a group.
group_concat(x)	Returns a string which is the concatenation of all non-NULL values of x
group_concat(x,y)	Returns a string which is the concatenation of all non-NULL values of x with the separator y
max(x)	Returns the maximum value of all values in the group.
min(x)	Returns the minimum non-NULL value of all values in the group.
sum(x)	Returns the sum of all non-NULL values in the group. If there are no non-NULL input rows it returns NULL.
total(x)	Returns the total of all non-NULL values in the group. If there are no non-NULL input rows then it returns 0.0.

You use the SELECT statement to perform these aggregate functions.

Let's illustrate aggregate functions with an example. Let's create a database with student's classwork, midterm and final marks as in Program 10.12.

Program 10.12
```
import sqlite3

# connection string
conn = sqlite3.connect('exam.db')
cursor = conn.cursor()

sql = """
CREATE TABLE exam (
stud_id INTEGER PRIMARY KEY,
stud_name VARCHAR(20),
classwork INTEGER,
midterm INTEGER,
final INTEGER); """

cursor.execute(sql)

mark = [ (1, 'sam', 20, 15, 40), (2, 'joe', 25, 18, 45),
         (3, 'sally', 24, 16, 42), (4, 'may', 28, 18, 42),
         (5, 'wong', 22, 15, 35), (6, 'chris', 16, 10, 20),
         (7, 'johnson', 28, 20, 48)]

# add the above 3 new products
cursor.executemany("""INSERT INTO exam (stud_id, stud_name, classwork,\
                   midterm, final) VALUES (?, ?, ?, ?, ?)""", mark)

cursor.execute("SELECT * FROM exam")
print('\n\t\tEXAM RESULTS\n')
result = cursor.fetchall()

print ('StudID\tStudName   Classwork  Midterm  Final   Total')

for rec in result:
    stud_id = rec[0]
    stud_name = rec[1]
    classwork = rec[2]
    midterm = rec[3]
    final = rec[4]
    total = classwork + midterm + final
    print ('  {}\t{}\t\t{}\t{}    \t{}\t{}'.format(stud_id, stud_name, \
```

```
                classwork, midterm, final, total))
conn.commit()
conn.close()
```

Output
```
                    EXAM RESULTS

StudID   StudName   Classwork   Midterm   Final
   1     sam            20        15       40
   2     joe            25        18       45
   3     sally          24        16       42
   4     may            28        18       42
   5     wong           22        15       35
   6     chris          16        10       20
   7     johnson        28        20       48
```

Program 10.13 uses the data in Program 10.12 to compute the average, maximum and minimum for the final mark using the aggregate functions avg, max and min.

Program 10.13
```
import sqlite3

conn = sqlite3.connect('exam.db')
cursor = conn.cursor()

q1 = """SELECT avg(final), max(final), min(final) FROM exam"""
cursor.execute(q1)
result = cursor.fetchone()
print ('(final avg, final max, final min)')
print (result)

conn.close()
```

Output
```
(final avg, final max, final min)
(38.857142857142854, 48, 20)
```

10.12 Multiple Database Tables

In all our examples so far, we have used only one database table. However, real applications would require multiple tables. SQLite, like other databases, allows you to have multiple tables in a database. This section tells how to work with multiple tables.

To illustrate, consider a simple employee database with just two tables: employee and department as follows:

employee

EmpID	EmpName	Dept	JobTitle	Salary
6	chris	MKT	Manager	5000
2	joe	HR	Manager	3500
7	johnson	HR	Exec	3700
4	may	IT	Programmer	4500
3	sally	AC	Exec	2700
1	sam	IT	Analyst	4900
5	wong	MKT	Exec	3200

department

Dept	Dept Name
IT	IT Services

```
HR        Human Resource
AC        Accounting
MKT       Marketing
```

Program 10.14 illustrates working with multiple tables. It creates a database (employee) with two tables (employee and department) and populates them using data from the lists emp and dep respectively.

Program 10.14
```python
import sqlite3
# connection string
conn = sqlite3.connect('employee.db')
cursor = conn.cursor()

# create and populate employee table from list emp

sql = """
CREATE TABLE employee (
emp_id INTEGER PRIMARY KEY,
emp_name VARCHAR(20),
dept VARCHAR(5),
job_title VARCHAR(15),
salary DECIMAL (7, 2)); """

cursor.execute(sql)

emp = [ (1, 'sam', 'IT', 'Analyst', 4900),
        (2, 'joe', 'HR', 'Manager', 3500),
        (3, 'sally', 'AC', 'Exec', 2700),
        (4, 'may', 'IT', 'Programmer', 4500),
        (5, 'wong', 'MKT', 'Exec', 3200),
        (6, 'chris', 'MKT', 'Manager', 5000),
        (7, 'johnson', 'HR', 'Exec', 3700)]

cursor.executemany("""INSERT INTO employee (emp_id, emp_name, dept,\
                   job_title, salary) VALUES (?, ?, ?, ?, ?)""", emp)

# create and populate department table from list dep

sql = """
CREATE TABLE department (
dept VARCHAR(5) PRIMARY KEY,
dept_name VARCHAR(20)); """

cursor.execute(sql)

dep = [ ('IT', 'Information Services'),
        ('HR', 'Human Resource'),
        ('AC', 'Accounting'),
        ('MKT', 'Marketing')]

cursor.executemany("""INSERT INTO department (dept, dept_name)\
                   VALUES (?, ?)""", dep)

# print the employee records
cursor.execute("SELECT * FROM employee")
print('\nEmployee details:')
result = cursor.fetchall()
print (result)

#print the department records
cursor.execute("SELECT * FROM department")
print('\nDepartments:')
result = cursor.fetchall()      # result is a list
```

```
print (result)
conn.commit()
conn.close()
```

Output
```
Employee details:
[(1, 'sam', 'IT', 'Analyst', 4900), (2, 'joe', 'HR', 'Manager', 3500), (3, 'sally',
'AC', 'Exec', 2700), (4, 'may', 'IT', 'Programmer', 4500), (5, 'wong', 'MKT',
'Exec', 3200), (6, 'chris', 'MKT', 'Manager', 5000), (7, 'johnson', 'HR', 'Exec',
3700)]

Departments:
[('IT', 'IT Services'), ('HR', 'Human Resource'), ('AC', 'Accounting'), ('MKT',
'Marketing')]
```

The above output (in list form) is not so readable, so let's reformat the output as in Program 10.15.

Program 10.15
```
import sqlite3
conn = sqlite3.connect('employee.db')
cursor1 = conn.cursor()

conn2 = sqlite3.connect('department.db')
cursor2 = conn.cursor()

cursor1.execute("SELECT * FROM employee")
result = cursor1.fetchall()

print('\nEmployee details:')
print ('EmpID\tEmpName\t\tDept\tJobTitle\tSalary')
for rec in result:
    emp_id = rec[0]
    emp_name = rec[1]
    dept = rec[2]
    job_title = rec[3]
    salary = rec[4]
    print (' {}\t{}\t\t{{}}\t{}     \t {}'.format(emp_id, emp_name, \
            dept, job_title, salary))

cursor2.execute("SELECT * FROM department")
result = cursor2.fetchall()
print('\nDepartments:')
print ('Dept\tDept Name')
for rec in result:
    dept = rec[0]
    dept_name = rec[1]
    print ('{}\t{}'.format(dept, dept_name))
conn.close()
```

Output
```
Employee details:
EmpID    EmpName          Dept    JobTitle       Salary
1        sam              IT      Analyst        4900
2        joe              HR      Manager        3500
3        sally            AC      Exec           2700
4        may              IT      Programmer     4500
5        wong             MKT     Exec           3200
6        chris            MKT     Manager        5000
7        johnson          HR      Exec           3700

Departments:
Dept    Dept Name
IT      Information Technology
```

185

```
HR        Human Resource
AC        Accounting
MKT       Marketing
```

The above two database tables – employee and department - are disjoint. They are not connected or related. Relational databases work by setting relationships between tables through *foreign keys*. The foreign key in one table allows information to be accessed from another table where that foreign key field is a *primary key*.

Program 10.16 illustrates this. The foreign key dept in the employee table references the primary key dept in the department table using the clause

```
FOREIGN KEY (dept) REFERENCES department (dept))
```

With this, you can access information in the department table from the employee table.

Note the SQL statement

```
SELECT emp_id, emp_name, department.dept_name, salary \
          FROM employee, department \
          WHERE employee.dept = department.dept;)
```

Note the following:

- The dept field in the field list is prefixed with the department name indicating that it is from that table.

- Only those records that satisfy the criteria employee.dept = department.dept are fetched.

Program 10.16
```
import sqlite3
conn = sqlite3.connect('employee.db')
cursor = conn.cursor()

sql = '''DROP TABLE employee;'''
cursor.execute(sql)

sql = '''DROP TABLE department;'''
cursor.execute(sql)

sql = """
CREATE TABLE employee (
emp_id INTEGER PRIMARY KEY,
emp_name VARCHAR(20),
dept VARCHAR(5) NOT NULL,   # NOT NULL means the field cannot be empty
job_title VARCHAR(15),
salary DECIMAL (7,2),
FOREIGN KEY (dept) REFERENCES department (dept));"""

cursor.execute(sql)
conn.commit()

emp = [ (1, 'sam', 'IT', 'Analyst', 4900), (2, 'joe', 'HR', \
        'Manager', 3500), (3, 'sally', 'AC', 'Exec', 2700), \
        (4, 'may', 'IT', 'Programmer', 4500),(5, 'wong', 'MKT', \
        'Exec', 3200), (6, 'chris', 'MKT', 'Manager', 5000), \
        (7, 'johnson', 'HR', 'Exec', 3700)]

cursor.executemany("""INSERT INTO employee (emp_id, emp_name, dept,\
                   job_title, salary) VALUES (?, ?, ?, ?, ?)""", emp)
```

```
sql = """
CREATE TABLE department (
dept VARCHAR(5) PRIMARY KEY,
dept_name VARCHAR(20)); """

cursor.execute(sql)

dep = [ ('IT', 'IT Services'), ('HR', 'Human Resource'), \
            ('AC', 'Accounting'), ('MKT', 'Marketing')]

cursor.executemany("""INSERT INTO department (dept, dept_name) VALUES \
            (?, ?)""", dep)
conn.commit()

cursor.execute("SELECT emp_id, emp_name, department.dept_name, salary \
            FROM employee, department \
            WHERE employee.dept = department.dept;")

result = cursor.fetchall()

print('\nEmployee details:')

print ('EmpID\tEmpName\t\tDept\t\t\tSalary')
for rec in result:
    emp_id = rec[0]
    emp_name = rec[1]
    dept = rec[2]
    dept = dept.strip()
    salary = rec[3]
    print ('{}\t{}\t\t{}\t\t\t{}'.format(emp_id, emp_name, \
            dept, salary))

conn.close()
```

Output
```
Employee details:
EmpID   EmpName     Dept                    Salary
1       sam         IT Services             4900
2       joe         Human Resource          3500
3       sally       Accounting              2700
4       may         IT Services             4500
5       wong        Marketing               3200
6       chris       Marketing               5000
7       johnson     Human Resource          3700
```

10.13 MySQL Database

So far, we used SQLite in all our discussion and illustration. But you can also use other database software such as MySQL, Sequel Server and Oracle. We will briefly mention how to use MySQL in Python. All other database software will be similar.

To use MySQL in Python, you import the PyMySQL module as follows:

```
import PyMySQL
```

Except for the connect arguments, everything else will be the same as shown in the code below.

```
import PyMySQL

# create a connection object
conn = PyMySQL.connect("localhost",…,"product" )

# create cursor object
cursor = conn.cursor()

# execute a query
cursor.execute("SELECT VERSION()")

# fetch a record
data = cursor.fetchone()
print ("database version : %s " % data)

# close the connection
conn.close()
```

Exercise

1. Create an employee database (employee) with table (employee) with fields as follows:

```
emp_id        integer    5 characters
emp_name      string     20 characters
sex           string     1 character (m, f)
birth_date    date       between 1970 and 2017
dept          string     10 characters (IT, HR, Finance, Marketing)
salary        float      2 decimal places
```

   (a) Populate the database with seven records.
   (b) Print all the records with all the fields in the table using suitable headings.
   (c) Print all the records with emp_id, emp_name and salary fields with suitable headings.
   (d) Print all the records for dept = IT
   (e) Print employees whose salary is more than 2000.
   (f) Print employees whose salary is between 2000 and 3000.
   (g) Print all the employees who are females born between 1990 and 2015.

2. Add the fields hours and rate (both of type float) to the employee table in (1)

   (a) Calculate the salary field (hours * rate).
   (b) Calculate the minimum, maximum and average salaries.
   (c) List all the salaries for dept = HR

3. Create an student database (student) with table (student) with fields as follows:

```
stud_id       integer    5 characters
stud_name     string     20 characters
sex           string     1 character (m, f)
birth_date    date       between 1990 and 2017
dept          string     10 characters (IT, Business, Law)
```

   (a) Populate the database with ten records.
   (b) Print all the male students with their details.
   (c) Print all the female students whose are more than 20 years old.
   (d) Print all students in the IT department
   (e) Print stud_id, stud_name and dept fields for all students.

4. Create a library database to perform the following tasks:

   (a) List all the titles (books) published after 2015.
   (b) List all the titles on Software Engineering.
   (c) List all the titles published by Pearson.
   (d) List the titles with price > 100.
   (e) List the minimum, maximum and average price of all the titles.

5. Create a library database with two tables – library and publisher - using the foreign key pcode (publisher code) to perform the following tasks:

   (a) List all the titles where publisher = McGraw Hill.
   (b) List all the titles where publisher = McGraw Hill and year > 2010.
   (c) List all the titles where title = Software Engineering and publisher = Pearson.
   (d) List all the titles where publisher = McGraw Hill and price is between 50 and 100.
   (e) List all the titles on Python Programming where publisher = McGraw Hill or Pearson.

References

1. Mark Summerfield, Programming in Python 3: A Complete Introduction to the Python Language

2. John Zelle, Python Programming: An Introduction to Computer Science

3. Eric Matthes, Python Crash Course: A Hands-On, Project-Based Introduction to Programming

4. Mark Lutz, Python Pocket Reference: Python In Your Pocket, O'Reilly

5. Brian Overland, Python Without Fear

6. http://www.onlineprogrammingbooks.com/python/

7. https://www.tutorialspoint.com/python3/index.htm

8. https://docs.python.org/3/tutorial/index.html

9. https://pythonprogramming.net/introduction-to-python-programming/

10. https://www.python.org/about/gettingstarted/

11. https://www.python-course.eu/python3_course.php

12. http://www.learnpython.org/